Henry Christmas

The Money Market

What it is, What it Does, And How it is Managed

Henry Christmas

The Money Market
What it is, What it Does, And How it is Managed

ISBN/EAN: 9783744725200

Printed in Europe, USA, Canada, Australia, Japan

Cover: Foto ©Suzi / pixelio.de

More available books at **www.hansebooks.com**

THE

MONEY MARKET:

WHAT IT IS, WHAT IT DOES, AND HOW IT IS MANAGED.

BY

HENRY NOEL-FEARN, F.R.S.

LONDON:
FREDERICK WARNE AND CO.
BEDFORD STREET, COVENT GARDEN.
1866.

TO

HENRY SYKES THORNTON, Esq.,

M.A., F.R.S.,

THIS SMALL VOLUME ON A GREAT SCIENCE

Is Dedicated,

AS A MARK OF ESTEEM AND REGARD.

PREFACE.

But few words can be needed by way of preface to so small and unpretending a work as this. Its object is to familiarise the public mind with the first principles of monetary science, to render the "City Articles" in our newspapers intelligible to the general reader, and by showing that its difficulties are more imaginary than real, to do somewhat towards cultivating a taste for the science itself. In all commercial schools, at least as much as this book contains ought to be known; and it is a matter of just reproach to us as an educated nation, that political economy, of which monetary science forms one of the most important branches, is so little studied.

H. N. F.

London, *June*, 1866.

CONTENTS.

CHAPTER I.

THE TERMS—MONEY—CURRENCY—THE MONEY MARKET, &c. &c.

What is a Pound?—Terminology—Meaning of the Terms Money, Currency—Money of Account—William the Conqueror—Difference between Money and Currency—Value and Price . . . . pp. 1—7

CHAPTER II.

ORIGIN AND VARIETIES OF MONEY—BARTER—COINAGE.

Ancient Money—The Patriarchal Age—System of Barter—Exchange Difficulties — Use of Bullion — Invention of Coinage—Lydian Coins—Names of Ancient and Modern Money—Coinage of Athens—Modern Coins—Base Coinage . . . . pp. 8—20

CHAPTER III.

OF PAPER-MONEY—CREDIT—COMMERCE AND ITS NECESSITIES.

Advance of Commerce—Features or a New Era—Navigation and Discovery—Transfer of Debt—Bills of Exchange—Mercantile Credit—Public Credit—Theories of Commerce—Paper Money—Convertible and Inconvertible Currency—Imports and Exports—Balance of Trade . . pp. 21—36

CHAPTER IV.

BANKS AND BANKING—PRINCIPLES AND PRACTICE.

Origin of Banking—Seizure of Money by Charles I.—Why Banks Fail—Early Theory of Banking—How Enlarged—What Business is Proper for a Banker—Frauds and Failures—Anecdotes . . . . pp. 37—50

CHAPTER V.

THE BANK OF ENGLAND AND ITS CHARTER.

Origin and Objects of the Bank of England—Its Early Success—Suspension of Cash Payments—The Restriction Act—Lord Stanhope's Act—Peel's Act of 1819—Ditto 1844—Convertible and Inconvertible Currency . . . . pp. 51—67

CHAPTER VI.

NATIONAL DEBTS OR OBLIGATIONS—ENGLISH AND FOREIGN.

How National Debts arose—Illustrated by Examples—Questions to be Solved—National and Governmental Obligations—Case of Prussia—Case of Virginia—Case of Greece—Supposed Beneficial Effect of a National Debt—The Case Examined . . . . pp. 68—82

CHAPTER VII.

PUBLIC FUNDS—CONSOLS—EXCHEQUER BILLS, ETC.

The Funds—Consols—Other Government Stock—The Unfunded Debt—Mediæval Loans—Revenue Anticipated—Irredeemable Debt—Acts of Consolidation—Perpetual Annuities—Dr. Price's Opinions—Variations in the Price of Stocks—Causes of such Variation . . . . pp. 83—93

CHAPTER VIII.

OF THE STOCK EXCHANGE—BROKERS—JOBBERS, ETC.

History and Business of the Stock Exchange—Mode of Transfer—Brokers, Jobbers, and Speculators—Bulls, Bears, and Lame Ducks—Time Bargains—High Character of the Stock Exchange—Nature and Manner of Gambling—Tragedy of the Money Market . . . . pp. 94—109

CHAPTER IX.

PRINCIPLES OF COMMERCE—FREE TRADE AND RESTRICTION.

Freedom of Commerce—Instances of—Necessity of Taxation—Employment of Duties—Retaliative Duties—Protective Duties—Chili Stockings—Corn Laws—How to be understood—Competition Rent—Colonial Produce—Commerce to be entirely Free . . . . pp. 110—121

CHAPTER X.

OF JOINT-STOCK COMPANIES AND LIMITED LIABILITY.

Necessity of New Legislation—Meaning of the term *Commandite*—Equity of the New Law—Real Liability—Large and Small Shares—Lord Overstone's Opinion—Progress of the Principle—Early Opposition—Joint-Stock Banks—Their Liability . . . . pp. 122—135

CHAPTER XI.

DISCOUNT AND FINANCE COMPANIES.

Nature of Discount Companies—Nature and Origin of Finance Companies—Their vast Designs—Examples from the Turkish Empire—Danger of distant Enterprises—Perils of Finance Companies—Aid to Railways—Prospects of the Principle . . . . pp. 136—148

CHAPTER XII.

PANICS AND THEIR CONSEQUENCES.

Nature of a Panic—Various Causes—Operations for the Fall—Bank Failures—How Caused—Hints to Shareholders—Effect of Wise Conduct on the part of the Public—Maxims of the late Duke of Wellington—Description of a Panic . . . . pp. 149—169

CHAPTER XIII.

HOW THE NATIONAL DEBTS ARE TO BE PAID.

Necessity of the Payment—Taxation—How to be Arranged—
—Direct and Indirect—Argument in favour of Each—Income Tax—Excise and Customs—Balance in favour of Taxation, partly Direct and partly Indirect . . . . pp. 170—178

CHAPTER XIV.

GREAT FINANCIAL FAMILIES.

Great Financial Families—The Houses of Coutts—Payne and Smith—Jones Loyd—Lord Overstone—The Barings—Lord Ashburton—The Rothschilds—Original Name Amschel—Origin of the name Rothschild—Nathan Rothschild.
pp. 179—192

CHAPTER I.

THE TERMS—MONEY—CURRENCY—THE MONEY MARKET, &c. &c.

What is a Pound?—Terminology—Meaning of the terms Money, Currency—Money of Account—William the Conqueror—Difference between Money and Currency, Value and Price.

THE late Sir Robert Peel startled the House of Commons into a remarkable confession of unconscious ignorance, by asking the apparently simple question—"What is a Pound?" It is probable that a great majority of persons considered well educated would feel as much embarrassed were they asked—What is money? and what is meant by the Money Market? They imagine that they are acquainted with all that is necessary on the subject, and are not aware how little they do know, till they come to take their knowledge to pieces. Of all sciences monetary science has been branded as at once the most dry and the most difficult, and the notion thus formed has deterred thousands from attempting its study. Yet the elements of the science are singularly interesting. To trace the causes which have led to the civilization of the world, to the greatness of nations, to the comforts and conveniences of life, cannot but be a fascinating employment; and like all other sciences, as its interest increases its difficulties diminish.

To prosecute this study with success, we must first clearly ascertain the real meaning of the terms in use. Half the difficulties which have agitated mankind have derived their origin from neglect in doing this. We shall commence this treatise, therefore, by explaining its terminology.

Money is a term applied, in the first place, to the circulating medium. Thus in our own country gold, silver, copper, and bank-notes are called by this name. In the second place, it is used to express whatever may be the representative of value or property, such as mercantile securities; and thus an individual may be said to be "a monied man," when what is meant is that he is a rich man, whose resources represent money, and can be converted into it at his pleasure. On the other hand, we should not apply the term to a man whose lands were extensive, or who was the master of many flocks and herds. Money, therefore, is a general term, signifying the circulating medium, or anything representing it.

The word "currency" differs from money in extent

—it signifies that which is accepted in any district as its circulating medium, its instrument of purchase and sale; and as that which is so accepted in one district is declined in another, " currency" is a more restricted term than "money:" it implies that which is subject to changes, to the operations of law and national custom. Thus, a Greek drachma or a Roman denarius will be a piece of money so long as it exists, but it is no longer currency. The authority which made it current—or, in other words, enabled it *" to run"*—has passed away. New rulers have superseded it, and have stamped other pieces to fill its place. Hence we have no word bearing the same relation to " currency ' that " monied" does to money.

There is yet another use of the word which is a relic of the barbarous ages of commerce. We still hear of "money of account." This is when the currency of a country and the mode of keeping accounts adopted by its merchants do not correspond. But we cannot call that money of account which, though it does not exist as a coin, is yet in accordance with the monetary system of the country. When William the Conqueror introduced into England the mode of reckoning by pounds, shillings, and pence, he did not introduce a mere money of account, because, though there were indeed neither pounds nor shillings, yet the penny, the only coin, was of such weight that two hundred and forty made up the Saxon pound, and twelve, therefore, the Saxon shilling. This was a convenience for reckoning, and nothing more.

But where the terms and system of an obsolete coinage are retained, and accounts are kept in accordance with it, and the circulating medium is modern—as if English merchants employed pounds, shillings, and pence in actual payments, but kept their accounts in marks and nobles—then we have that which is with strictness called money of account. The mark "*lubs*"—that is, the mark of Lubeck, 14¾d. of our money—in the terms of which accounts are kept in Hamburg, is a case in point; and there is more intricacy in these accounts and in settling the rate of exchange between Hamburg and other countries in consequence of this relic of barbarism. Indeed, the whole German currency is a puzzle for the unpractised— a puzzle as intricate as the money itself is disagreeable.

"THE MONEY MARKET," again, is a term which sometimes occasions a great amount of perplexity to the uninitiated; for, to those who consider money solely as the instrument by which purchases and sales are effected, to buy or sell money must appear an unintelligible expression. We must bear in mind that time and distance are elements in our calculation. Thus, I have a promissory note from A. B. to pay me £100 at three months' date. I want the money *now*. I *buy* it, therefore, with A. B.'s note; and the difference between £100 and the sum I receive for the note is the price I pay for the accommodation. On the other hand, the purchaser or "*discounter*" of the note buys with a sum of money short of £100 the right of receiving £100 at the end of three months. Here time and money are the elements of the transaction. In like manner, I may introduce the element of distance. With £105 I may bargain, at a certain date, to receive £110 at Madrid.

The money market exists, therefore, wherever monetary transactions are carried on, and the term signifies the *rationale* of such transactions over the whole mercantile world. When money is abundant, the market is said to be "*easy;*" when it is scarce, the market is "*tight.*" It is affected by peace and war, by diplomacy and politics, as well as by commerce; and it affects in turn public and private credit; mercantile and individual interests. It aids or hinders enterprise, and is, generally speaking, the gauge of commercial prosperity.

Two other terms, of an abstract nature, require a few words of explanation; these are "value" and "price." Value, as a term in ordinary use, implies utility; a thing is valuable according as it is useful. Air, fire, health, life, energy, morality, are valuable, because without some of these we cannot live happily; without others we cannot live at all; but they are of no direct value in the money market, where the term is solely used in the sense of that market. If a man could sell his share in the July sunshine, or his right to breathe the common air, then these would have "value"— that is, they would become marketable and susceptible of price. "Value," then, is the worth of anything expressed in monetary terms; and "price," the amount realizable at any given time. Commodities are frequently sold above, and frequently below, their value. I select, as an instance, Spanish bonds. The real value of these instruments is very difficult to ascertain; it depends on many contingencies. I incline to rate it highly. The immense resources of the country, the general tone of feeling in the Spanish nation, the probability that the Spanish Government will have to apply to the European markets for loans—and those of considerable extent—and the certainty that this can only be done successfully by a nation which keeps faith with its creditors, induce me to form this opinion as to the *value* of these bonds. Their *price* is, however, very low—much under their nominal value.

We shall now proceed to consider the nature and *value* of money.

CHAPTER II.

ORIGIN AND VARIETIES OF MONEY—BARTER—COINAGE.

Ancient Money—The Patriarchal Age—System of Barter—Exchange Difficulties—Use of Bullion—Invention of Coinage—Lydian Coins—Names of Ancient and Modern Money—Coinage of Athens—Modern Coins—Base Coinages.

THERE are few questions connected with political economy more surrounded with difficulties than what is called the "currency question," and there are few about which greater errors prevail. Of these, one of the greatest, perhaps the greatest of all, is that which confounds wealth with money— an error all the more serious from its almost universal diffusion. A little attention to the etymological meaning of words would help us greatly in this and many other matters. Wealth is a Saxon word, and signifies that which consitutes our *well-being*. We speak of the *commonwealth*, or common *weal*, which is a more comprehensive term than the Roman *res-publica,* and applies not only to the possession, but also to the happiness of the body politic. Another phrase shows us that the opposite of weal or wealth is not poverty, but *woe*. Riches and poverty are correlative terms, but wealth and poverty are not so. But neither may riches be confounded with money, nor the want of money be considered synonymous with poverty. What, then, is money? Money is the circulating medium. It may be gold, silver, and copper, as in civilized Europe; it may be tin, as in the Birman empire; it may be shells, as on the coast of Africa; or it may be salt, as in the interior of the same continent; but whatever form it may assume, it is the current representative of value. Were there no such thing as money, all the products of the earth would have to be bartered one for the other; the division of labour would be all but impossible, and trade could hardly exist. Let us take a familiar instance: A boat-builder has constructed a boat; he wants boots; a bootmaker can supply him with boots, but he does not want the boat, which is all the builder has to offer, nor does the builder require so many boots as will make up the value of the boat. Both, then, must wait till they find other parties with other goods, by means of which, through a series of barters, the builder may dispose of his boat and obtain his boots. Now, all this is done by a simple transaction when money is used. It acts, in the first place, as a universal measure of value; so that, instead of saying one boat is equal to thirty pairs of boots, and one leg of mutton is equal to ten and a half four-pound loaves, we say the boat is worth £30 sterling, the pair of boots is worth one pound, the leg of mutton is worth seven shillings, and the four-pound loaf is worth eightpence; secondly, it renders ordinary barter needless, for the boat-builder is able to sell his boat at once to the person who requires it, and with the *money* to buy boots, and whatever else he requires instead. Yet this is but a new and more convenient kind of barter, after all; instead of obtaining bread, meat, boots, coats, and a cottage, directly in exchange for so many boats, he obtains a certain amount of silver and gold, which in his turn he barters for the necessaries of life. Or, to take a step deeper still, the money is a common measure, which, in the great division of productive labour, enables him to barter his own for that of his fellows.

The necessity of some kind of currency would arise in a very early state of civilization. The division of labour would require some measure of value; this must soon become a common measure, and actual barter would speedily take a more complicated but more convenient form, by making this common measure to serve as a circulating medium. Mankind was not long in deciding that the precious metals formed by far the most convenient material for such a medium; they are subject to little fluctuation of value: they are durable, extremely divisible, and of small bulk; they readily take and long retain the impress of any stamp made upon them, and thus may easily be rendered representatives of any amount of current value. Again, they are not a merely fictitious standard; the coin which I call a sovereign does not derive its value solely from the amount at which it is fixed by the Government; for if I melt it, or cut it in pieces, I can procure with it nearly as much of any commodity. It is intrinsically worth what I buy with it, and the same may be said of all the coins of this realm; they are, in fact, valuables, capable of being bartered for other valuables, and by their divisions and subdivisions, extremely convenient for the purpose.

The civilization of Egypt was the first, so far as we can discover, which adopted and enjoyed the inevitably beneficial results of this expedient. Commercial dealings gradually became smaller in the individual transaction, but larger on the whole, as men were gathered into cities, and the division of labour more complete. Rings of gold and silver, adjusted to a certain weight and fineness, and strung on cords by certain numbers, supplied for ages the requisite currency. These rings saved all the trouble of weighing and dividing; they could be made small enough for daily purchases, and so far possessed all the advantages of a coinage properly so called; but on the other hand they might be easily counterfeited, and their weight and quality had to be taken on the authority of him who offered them. The touchstone and the scales were occasionally necessary, and all purchases seemed to require the weighing as well as the counting of the rings; thus much we gather from Egyptian monuments. Cæsar, describing the currency used in Britain before his invasion, speaks of rings graduated to a certain weight as forming an important part of it. He mentions indeed only iron as so used; but, as in Ireland, gold and silver rings, very carefully adjusted as to their weight, have been found in considerable numbers, and as it appears certain that they were used as currency, it seems most probable that such was the case also in our own island. To this day small bars of silver, bent into a half circle, and called fish-hook money, pass current in Ceylon; these, however, are stamped with certain Cingalese characters, and are always of the same weight (68 grains); so that they are in fact coins, and only differ from those more commonly used by the peculiarity of their shape.

The names given anciently to money are very suggestive; some indicate weight or quality, and others value or wealth. The earliest with which we are acquainted occurs in the book of Genesis, xxxiii. 19, where Jacob is said to have bought a part of a field from the children of Hamor for a hundred pieces of money; but the word used has been translated "*a lamb.*" Coined money was not in use for many centuries later; and the question arises whether the bullion was marked with the figure of a lamb, or whether lambs themselves were the medium of barter. The same expression occurs in the book of Job, xiii. 11, where friends are described as giving him each one a "lamb," or "a piece of money" so marked; but the word there used, "*kesitah*," signifies a portion, and the whole argument as to the stamp of a lamb thus falls to the ground. There is, however, nothing improbable in "*portions*" of silver having such a stamp, and being called by such a name, just as, in subsequent periods, we find masses of lead or iron cast into the shape of a pig, and called respectively pigs of lead or iron. The *kesitah*, as a coin, belonged to Cyprus, and was not struck till B.C. 450. The Roman *pecunia*, signifying *cattle*, did certainly indicate the patriarchal condition, in which the wealth of the rich consisted in flocks and herds; and some of the earliest pieces are, in consideration of this, marked with an ox. *Money* is derived from "*monere*," to advise or instruct—an etymology less obvious than the rest. It arose from a tradition that the first coins were struck in the Temple of Juno Moneta or the adviser. The shekel is a weight, from *sakal*, to weigh; the *stater* has a similar meaning, as also has the *drachma*, with its multiples and divisions; but the original meaning of *drachma* is a *handful*, six oboli being considered a handful, and going to make up the drachma. The *obolus* is a small spike, or nail. In modern times, the terms *cash, rapp, doit, stiver,* used to represent money in general—and in the three last cases very small sums—are, in fact, names of coins all extant. The words gold, silver, brass, tin, have in all languages, and in all ages, been used with more or less elegance for money, as indicating the material of which the circulating medium was composed; and the devices on coins have served to give denominations to pieces, apart from their actual value; thus we have the crown, the sovereign, the noble, the rial, the écu, or shield, the lion, the eagle, and of old, the owl, the tripod, &c.

The pecuniary transactions recorded in the Bible were all, we can scarcely doubt, effected by means of bullion, the shekel being simply a recognised weight. One remarkable proof of this will be found in the history of Joseph. On the return of his brethren from Egypt, each man, on opening his sack of corn, found his "*bundle of money*," Gen. xliii. 21, in the mouth of his sack. The pictures in Sir Gardiner Wilkinson's work on Egypt show, as we have already seen, that the "*bundles*" of money consisted of rings of silver or gold tied together; and that this custom, or something analogous to it, continued till after the captivity, is plain from the words of Jeremiah, xxxii. 9: "And I bought the field of Hanameel, my uncle's son, that was in Anathoth, and weighed him the money, seventeen shekels of silver." At this time, however, there can be little doubt that coined money was beginning to find its way into Jerusalem.

These passages and several others seem to indicate that silver, ready cut and weighed, furnished the currency of the Israelites during the long period comprehended between the time of Abraham and that of Saul, and that, for a considerable time after, no great change took place, is equally clear; but at what period coined money was introduced it is difficult to say. Up to the time of Saul the value of men and cattle seems to have been computed in "*pieces of silver.*" Gold was probably reserved for personal ornament. Thus we find Pharaoh casting a gold chain round the neck of Joseph; and we hear of jewels of gold, as well as jewels of silver, among the "*spoils*" which the Israelites brought away from their Egyptian captivity.

Of gold used as money we have only one early instance recorded in Scripture, and that as late as the time of David: "He bought the threshing-floor, cattle, and agricultural implements of Ornan, the Jebusite, for six hundred shekels of gold, 'by weight,' " 1 Ch. xxi. 25. It must, however, be borne in mind that the transaction is differently related in the second book of Samuel, and that the price paid for the threshing-floor and cattle is said to be fifty shekels of silver, 2 Sam. xxiv. 24.

The exigencies of commerce soon required a currency which might pass unquestioned, might admit of subdivisions minute enough to serve for the smallest purposes, and might render imitation, if not impossible, at least a difficult achievement. The common sense of mankind ·point out that sovereignties alone, however constituted, could exercise advantageously the right of striking coins on this principle, and that the security of the public required that it should be committed to no other hands. The piece of metal stamped with the symbol indicating the recognised authority of the State would, as a matter of course, pass unquestioned within the limits of that State, and the counterfeiting it would be severely punished. At the same time, there must be a close approximation between the actual and the nominal value; if the coin be worth much less than it claims to be, it will, in spite of all penalties, be extensively counterfeited, even in fine metal. If it be worth a little more, it will speedily disappear from circulation. And this approximation must be very close indeed if the coin be intended to circulate beyond the State in which it is struck. Thus, the early Athenian silver currency passed not only all over Greece, but round all the shores of the Mediterranean. And when the growth and progress of art made the home coinage of Athens so beautiful that it has never yet been equalled, the pieces intended for foreign circulation were obliged to be struck in the same rude archaic form in which they had at first obtained the confidence of barbarous nations.

It is a singular circumstance that, to satisfy a

similar requisition in Africa and the remote East, dollars are struck in Spain and Austria bearing respectively the dates and portraits of Charles III. and Maria Theresa.

The early materials for coins were gold, silver, and electrum—a beautiful metal, formed by a mixture of gold and silver. It seems at first to have been a natural amalgam and afterwards made by art.

Coined metal was probably an invention of the Lydians, though there is necessarily a considerable doubt on the subject. Herodotus gives the earliest gold coinage to that people, and we hear of no other coins till a much later period. Pheidon, of Argos, according to the Parian Chronicle, first coined silver in the island of Ægina. But the date of this is very uncertain; according to the marble at 895 before Christ; according to Böckh, Clinton, and Müller, from 783 to 744; and according to Grote from 770 to 730. If we take the first of these periods, and suppose Pheidon to have been the inventor of coinage, then the art will be coeval with the reign of Jehoshaphat; if the last, with that of Hezekiah. The question of priority between Lydia and Greece is one which is never likely to be accurately decided. We, however, judge the earliest coins extant to be of about the eighth century before the Christian era. Whether of gold or silver, they are mere shapeless lumps of metal, having on the obverse some design more or less rude and archaic in character; and on the reverse, one or more cavities, being the impression or impressions of a punch. It is by no means improbable that Crœsus struck gold coins, and that some of the gold coins found about Sardis may be the coinage of that wealthy monarch. These were called *staters,* from a Greek word signifying *"a standard,"* and the term was afterwards applied to all coins in gold of the size and weight corresponding to the drachma, and in silver to the tetra-drachma.

It will be unnecessary to dwell longer on the denominations of coin, and its employment in ancient times; a few words on the base coins of modern Europe will conclude this chapter. Faith has not always been kept with the public in the matter of coinage. In many countries the currency has been depreciated to an extent disgraceful to the government which perpetrated the fraud, and to the age in which it was tolerated. In our own country, the reigns of Henry VIII., Edward VI., and Mary were signalized by this barbarous and dishonourable expedient. Elizabeth, while she abolished it in England, continued it in Ireland, but from the time of James I., the currency of this country has always been of good metal, as it was from the first coinages of the Anglo-Saxon kings to the latter end of the reign of Henry VIII.

The condemnation which we apply to this miserable expedient, is not shared by those coinages of mixed metal which yet prevail in Germany, and some other parts of the continent of Europe. They are dirty, greasy, and unpleasant, both to the touch and the sight, but they are not dishonest; they do not pass for silver; they are ugly, however, and inconvenient, and the sooner they are " reformed " away from the face of the earth, the better for all concerned.

CHAPTER III.

OF PAPER-MONEY—CREDIT—COMMERCE AND ITS NECESSITIES.

Advance of Commerce—Features of a New Era—Navigation and Discovery—Transfer of Debt—Bills of Exchange—Mercantile Credit—Public Credit—Theories of Commerce—Paper Money—Convertible and Inconvertible Currency—Imports and Exports—Balance of Trade.

WHEN the great step had been taken of establishing a metallic currency, it seemed as if all the possible requisitions of commerce were provided for, and for a while, indeed for many centuries, nothing more was needed,—but as in process of time the necessities of trade advanced, as distant lands were brought within the sphere of mercantile operations; more especially after a way had been found to India, round by the Cape of Good Hope, and America had been added to the dominions of trade, the old modes of communication proved insufficient. It will be clear too, that contact with an older, though more imperfect civilization, must have had some effect on the commercial operations of Europe. India and China exercised their influence in this way, while the impulse given to enterprise and speculation was increased tenfold by the Reformation, and the invention of printing. The whole world was wakened up to the life of a new era, and Portugal, Spain, and Venice took the lead in the mercantile operations of the rising age. Then it was that paper-money was felt to be the currency which the time required. Book-keeping became a science, and commerce assumed her due place in the agencies of civilization. The first and simplest operation, according to the new system, was the transfer of debt; the making a simple acknowledgment of a debt from A to B, a negotiable instrument. It is impossible to say at what time this simple transfer became common; isolated instances must have taken place at a very early period; but it required a large commercial community, of which the chief members were well known one to another, to make what may be called a credit circulation possible.

The purchase by gold or silver is a reliance on the actual wealth of the individual, and in point of fact, is but a barter of one commodity against another of equal value, but more convenient bulk; but if A says to B, I will give you an acknowledgment of my debt to you, and will pay you at the end of three months, and in the meantime you can transfer the acknowledgment to another person, and thus have the same advantages as though I had paid you; we have the introduction of a new system.

Now, if under these circumstances A is sufficiently well known to make his acknowledgment of equal value with the actual sum, we have all that is required, so far as he is concerned, to establish a paper currency. There are hundreds and thousands of men so thoroughly known in all commercial circles at the present time, that their acknowledgments would pass through the mercantile world as money. The general credit of all these collectively, makes up what is called *mercantile* credit—add to this, faith in the honesty of governments and the resources of nations, and we have what is commonly denominated *public* credit.

The common system of shopkeeping is one of the simplest forms of ordinary credit; it is very ancient, and is hardly susceptible of much improvement. It is inconvenient for those who require continual but moderate supplies to pay cash for all the small articles they want at the time of sending for them; it would be still more inconvenient to be obliged to purchase in large quantities. Thus the shopkeeper became a distributor and at the same time a creditor, and the consumer a debtor, the profits of the shop in the first place being measured by the difference between the wholesale and the retail prices of the commodities dealt in. The shopkeeper therefore sells his time and labour, and expends capital in the keeping up of his shop and in all the minor expences connected with it, receiving the above-named difference as his payment, and setting the credit given by him to his customers, and that received by him from manufacturers and wholesale dealers, the one against the other.

From this simple form of credit we advance upwards till we come, by easy transitions, to operations involving millions of money, and the names and reputations of the greatest capitalists.

On this public credit the members of the mercantile class draw, and on the whole the system is found to work well, to supply all the requisite facilities for carrying on the world's business, and to be accompanied by (comparatively speaking) so few failures, as not to give cause for any harassing suspicion. It is understood that honesty is the best policy, and most men know that others understand it to be so. Frauds, forgeries, and failures always will occur, but their proportion is small compared with the amount of *bonâ fide* business, and the best authorities are of opinion that the proportion is rather on the decrease than otherwise. Indeed the great advance in the means of communication which modern times supply is in itself a hindrance to fraud. Science is employing its powers as well to repress as to forward it, with this difference, that the effects of science in this respect are permanent for good and transient for evil. Newspapers, the telegraph, photographs, and many other ways of conveying intelligence, are every day more and more used. Publicity is recognised as one of the chief requisites of commerce. The *value* of a bill bearing the names of Baring or Rothschild depends upon the actual solvency of those capitalists, but its *usefulness* depends on the general knowledge which mercantile men have of their solvency. Were a series of misfortunes to occur to a man of such a class, so far as these misfortunes were extensively known, so far his credit would suffer and his bills be less negotiable; yet it might be that every one of these instruments would have precisely the same real value, and be paid at the time when it became due without the slightest delay. A credit circulation requires constant publicity, and can only exist where the fullest liberty of communication exists likewise.

The old notion of commerce was, that it consists

in knowing how to buy as cheaply and to sell as dearly as possible, and this required little communication among nations. The price of an article was made to depend on the need of the buyer and the greed of the seller, and nothing else was taken into consideration. This notion even still prevails in the East; and though more lofty and scientific principles are slowly making their way among the honest Turks and the crafty Chinese, the intellectual Hindoos, and the versatile Persians, still the ancient principle or no principle governs the majority, and will take many years still to root out.

But commerce in civilized nations is regarded from a totally different point of view—it is no longer the mere art, or rather "knack," of buying cheap and selling dear. It is a great science—the object of which is to take all the productions of nature, and to distribute them over the surface of the globe—or, as a well-known writer has expressed it, to take the various gifts of our common Father, and distribute them among His great human family. A very good definition declares it to be the science of distribution. Regarded under this aspect, credit becomes an important part of commerce, and without this, commerce would soon go back to metallic payments and barter. It is by credit alone that trade can be freely carried on between distant nations; and the less necessity there is for bullion, the more rapidly and more easily are its objects accomplished.

The great instrument of modern commerce is the Bill of Exchange, and this is described as follows by Mr. Gilbart:—

A bill of exchange is a written order from one person to another, directing him to pay a sum of money either to the drawer or to a third person at a future time. This is usually a certain number of days, weeks, or months, either after the date of the bill, or after sight; that is, after the person on whom it is drawn shall have *seen* it, and shall have written on the bill the word "*Accepted,*" and his name. If the bill be drawn after sight, he also writes the date of the acceptance.

Besides their utility as a means of transferring money from one place to another, bills have the following advantages:—

They are a means of transferring debts from one person to another. If I owe a man £100, and another man owes me £100, I will draw a bill for that amount on my debtor, and give it to my creditor. I have thus transferred the debt from my debtor to my creditor, and my own debt is liquidated. My debtor, instead of paying me the money he owed me, will pay it to the holder of the bill. My creditor will now look for payment to my debtor, and consider me simply as a guarantee for the payment of the bill. If he wishes to make use of the bill, he will again transfer the debt to another party, placing his own name on the bill as an additional guarantee. The bill may thus pass through a variety of hands and liquidate a great number of debts, before it becomes due. When due, it will be paid by the acceptor who was the original debtor, and all these intermediate transactions will be closed.

Bills fix the period for the payment of debts, and in case of litigation they afford an easy proof of the debt. A person will have little scruple in putting off a tradesman to whom he owes money, and the creditor dares not be urgent, lest the debtor should no longer deal with him; hence the time of payment can never be calculated upon with certainty. But if the customer has given a bill for the amount he owes, that bill will circulate into the hands of other persons who will be more peremptory in demanding payment, and whose applications cannot be disregarded with impunity.

Bills afford an easy mode of giving a guarantee. A person may wish to borrow money of me, and I may be unwilling to lend it to him, unless he procure a more wealthy person to guarantee the repayment at a given time. If he has a friend that will do this, the most easy way of effecting the guarantee is by means of a bill drawn by the borrower upon his friend. This, in point of security, is the same thing as a letter of guarantee; but it has also this additional advantage, that if I should want the money before the time fixed for its repayment, I can get this bill discounted, and reimburse myself the money I have advanced. Bills of this description are called accommodation-bills, or wind-bills, or kites. When employed only as a means of affording occasional assistance to a needy friend, or for raising a sum of money for a short time, to meet an unexpected call, they do not appear to be very objectionable. But when systematically pursued for the purpose of raising fictitious capital whereon to trade, they uniformly indicate the folly and effect the ruin of all the parties concerned.

A curious anecdote is related of an eminent judge recently deceased, illustrative of these terms. When yet a junior, he had to refer to some questionable proceedings of this kind, and observed: "Now, gentlemen of the jury, the unfortunate defendant had been amusing himself by flying kites."

"Doing what?" interrupted the judge.

"Flying kites, my lord—putting his name to accommodation-bills."

"Why are they called kites?" inquired the judge.

"Why, my lord, as in the case of schoolboys' kites, there is a connexion between the kite and the wind—only there the wind raises the kite, and here the kite raises the wind."

But all this indicates that the paper or credit circulation is convertible, that the notes or promises are promises to pay at a given time and in metallic currency. If the gold be not forthcoming, or is not supposed to be forthcoming *at the appointed time*, the bill is not negotiable, and becomes a mere piece of waste paper. The next step, therefore, in the progress of monetary science is to establish a currency which shall actually take the place of *money*—shall be independent of the personal credit of individuals, and shall be payable on demand. This so far approaches an inconvertible currency, that it may be made a legal tender—that is, not to be refused when offered for payment. No man can be compelled to accept payment for his rent in bills of the first merchants on 'Change, but if bank-notes are offered he must be satisfied. Yet these bank-notes are but promises on the part of a company of merchants to pay, on demand, the sum which they represent. The persons who would refuse to accept a bill on Rothschild *as money*, will gladly receive notes for which a company are responsible, not one member of which has half the wealth of the great Hebrew. In fact, law and custom have made the note *cash*, the bill is only so among those who know the enormous capital of the issuer.

The new principle is applied as follows:—

I give my tailor, in exchange for a suit of clothes, a piece of fine paper, the intrinsic value of which is too small to be easily expressed, and he not only accepts this, but gives me in addition to my suit of clothes many pieces of intrinsically valuable gold and silver. How is this? The paper is a banknote, and the tailor knows that by presenting it to its issuers, he shall receive as many sovereigns as it is stated to be worth; it is, in fact, a token or pledge, and its value must manifestly depend upon the credit of those who issue it. Were it known that the Bank could not redeem it, it would no longer have any marketable value; if any doubts arose on the subject, and these doubts could not at once be satisfied, it would be depreciated in proportion; it is a promissory note payable on demand. The advantages of a paper currency are, its portability and convenience of transmission, and its enabling large masses of specie to be advantageously enjoyed in other directions. A paper currency is of two kinds, convertible and inconvertible; it is convertible when those who issue it are bound to exchange it for specie on demand; and it is inconvertible when they are not so bound. An inconvertible currency prevailed for many years in this country; but, after many struggles and much discussion, the principle was abandoned as an unsound one, and the convertible paper substituted.

The arguments on both sides would require too much space to be admissible in an elementary book like the present, and may be found, moreover, considered at length in Mill's "Political Economy."

We come now to the consideration of what used to be called "*the balance of trade.*" This theory taught, as an axiom, that the advantage of foreign commerce lay chiefly in exports; and that in proportion as these exceeded the imports, in like manner the country became rich; just in the same way as a man who sells much and buys little accumulates money. But this fallacy depends on that already noticed, that money is wealth; were this the case, any government might become rich *ad libitum*, by simply increasing an inconvertible paper currency; but such a government would be soon taught that

> "The value of a thing
> Is just as much as it will bring,"

and that they could not grow rich by multiplying money.

Setting aside for the present all the higher advantages of commerce, its power of civilizing and refining, we must look to the actual benefits which it confers on a country; and these will be found to consist in what it brings in, not what it takes out; bullion must be regarded just as any other commodity, and if the whole value of the imports be greater than the whole value of the exports the country must be necessarily a gainer. A few words as to the way in which foreign business is transacted may help the reader to a more accurate understanding of this question. In large operations there is often little, if any, cash payment. A. sends from Bordeaux wine to the value of 1000 francs to B. in London; B. has sent a quantity of cotton cloth to C. at Bordeaux, worth £40; A. receives the 1000 francs from C., and the transaction is closed; or B. may send bills, that is, promises to pay money in France, and A. is paid with that which has in like manner been given in payment to B.: thus a mercantile transaction in one land is made to balance a similar transaction in another. Even travellers for pleasure often regulate their payments unconsciously in the same way. I go to spend a month with my friends in Spain; I pay £50 into the hands of my banker, who furnishes me with circular notes; thus I take out of the country neither gold nor silver, but only pieces of paper; for these I receive Spanish gold at Madrid, or Cadiz, or Barcelona, and my pieces of paper are made circuitously to pay for British manufactures exported into Spain.

And here may be a proper place to speak of the doctrine of exchanges. The nature of a bill of exchange has been already explained, but as the bill has to be paid in the currency of the country to which it is ultimately transmitted, it will be necessary to take into consideration the real value of the currency in the two countries. For instance, the Mint regulations of London and Paris agree as to the value of their respective coinages—say that the sovereign shall be worth 25 francs and 20 centimes —and when a sovereign in Paris purchases exactly this sum, and this sum in London purchases a sovereign, then the exchange is said to be *at par*.

But many causes may disturb this equality, for, first, it rarely happens that the coins of any country come up precisely to their strict legal standard either in weight or quality—some coins and some coinages are much worn, some are debased to a greater or less degree, not sufficient to injure their value as a circulating medium, but quite enough to cause their substitution as far as possible for the more pure and weighty coinages. If this tendency be not checked, the latter will disappear from circulation and a loss will be occasioned to that country which issued it. Thus, as the English sovereign is a well-known and popular coin, and rarely deviates much from its legal standard, the exchange is frequently in favour of England on this account. Bank-notes share the advantage because they are merely promises to pay on demand so many sovereigns.

But again, from various causes, there may be a divergence from the equality of exchange even when the purity of the metal is not called in question at all. Gold must be somewhat cheaper in California or in Australia, and silver in Mexico, than either metal can be in London, so that exchange between these countries may be really *at par* though nominally against the one which produces the precious metals. The depreciation of paper currency, the advance or decline of public credit, the state of trade in one country as compared with that in another, all influence the rate of exchange. The great agent, however, in all this fluctuation is the influx or efflux of bullion. All monetary transactions, though carried on by means of paper, have a metallic basis, and if this metallic basis be increasing in any country, then the exchange is in favour of that country—if decreasing, the reverse. Hence arises the interest with which men engaged in commerce regard the daily accounts of bullion brought into the country, and transmitted abroad; and hence the care with which all transactions of this kind, and especially those of the Bank of England, are chronicled.

CHAPTER IV.

BANKS AND BANKING—PRINCIPLES AND PRACTICE.

Origin of Banking—Seizure of Money by Charles I.—Why Banks Fail—Early Theory of Banking—How Enlarged—What Business is Proper for a Banker—Frauds and Failures—Anecdotes.

THE practice of banking arose in the first place from a feeling of insecurity as to the safe keeping of money. In the seventeenth century merchants sent it to the Tower, fancying it safer there than in their own strong boxes; but on this point, as well as on several others, they were undeceived by Charles I., who, having been refused a loan by the City of London, seized upon £200,000 lodged by merchants in the Mint (which was then established in the Tower), and compelled them to consider the robbery as a loan. The first banks were merely banks of deposit; but soon they began in one way or another to utilize these deposits, and to issue notes on their own authority.

So long as they did not go beyond this first intention, banks were at once safe and profitable.

They seem to have been known in ancient times, though we are unable to decide on what principle they were established, or to what extent they carried their operations. Nor is it our object to expatiate upon banking in the middle ages, or in other lands; our limits will compel us to confine our remarks to our own country, and as far as possible to our own time.

We have had so many failures of late that the uninitiated are inclined to think that there must be something extremely "rotten in the state of banking." What business *has* a bank to break? Such is the question hundreds are asking, in various tones of fear, anger, astonishment, and inquiry. Theoretically speaking, the reply is—None whatever. Practically—Very little, and that little very rarely. So that if a bank does, to use the popular phrase, "break," it may be presumed that its business has been either unskilfully or dishonestly conducted; and it will usually be found that the true cause of its failure has been a combination of the two. The primary idea of banking is at once a safe and a simple one. Merchants found it disadvantageous to keep large sums by them, and out of a chest of bullion to pay small accounts. It obviously would be a great step towards the emancipation of commerce, from minute and constantly recurring restrictions, if one person would undertake to keep the floating capital of a number of others, and to pay on demand such portions as might be required. The money itself was safer, because the necessary protection was unremitting and sufficient; and it was more economical, because it was quite as easy to hold against robbers a million as a thousand pounds. The merchant had the advantage of making his payments by simple slips of paper, had no anxiety about the safety of his floating capital, a great temptation to dishonesty was removed, and the transaction of business became at once all the easier and all the safer. But, supposing this safe and simple idea reduced to practice, what gain would accrue to the banker? He received from his customers—they were not called clients in those days—certain specific sums, which he was to return without deduction. He would have in the meantime to keep a staff of clerks, a shop—for so it was then termed—to give up his own time and attention, and to support his family, as well as to make a provision for the future, by his business. To secure this, and thereby give the commercial world the inestimable advantage of the banking system, it was absolutely necessary that the balances left in his hands should fructify. Out of the gain thus produced his profit was to accrue.

It was the payment made to him by the merchants and others whom he accommodated.

Thus, then, the business of a banker, *pur et simple*, becomes clearly defined. He is to be always ready to answer any demand made on him to the extent of the deposits which he has received. But it soon became clear that these demands would be limited to a tolerably well-defined proportion of the deposits; and that, except under extraordinary circumstances, one-fourth of the deposits would be sufficient to satisfy the claims. Three-fourths, therefore, of the money in his hands could be employed so as to produce a profit to himself; but to render this employment legitimate, it must be vested in securities easily and rapidly convertible, and not subject to any great fluctuation in the market. If this rule were attended to, the failure of a bank would be practically an impossibility, save only in the case of a long-continued and violent panic—and then it would be highly improbable. Let us, for instance, suppose a bank established in England by Messrs. Slowboy and Safe. They receive deposits in the course of a year to the extent of one million sterling; they keep one quarter of this to answer all demands made upon them, and invest the rest in Government securities, and thus there will accrue a gain of more than £25,000; for if the signs of a panic appear in the mercantile horizon, it would certainly in the first place affect houses of an inferior position; so that Messrs. Slowboy and Safe would have ample time to prepare for the storm. Moreover, their securities being of the highest order, easily and rapidly convertible into cash, and seldom affected to any ruinous extent by the fluctuations of the market, they would "ride out" a long pressure with scarcely any injury, and their depositors would suffer no loss. When the panic passed away, they would reap the advantage of their prudence in an increase of business.

This is the simplest, if not the earliest, *theory* of banking; and if rigidly adhered to, would warrant the query: What business has a bank to break? But it was hardly to be expected that a system so simple, even if ever reduced to practice, could remain in its simplicity. We have supposed two partners, and both devoted to their business as bankers. Now let us add another element, which, even in the earliest days of banking, was rarely absent; that of separate and independent business. Mr. Slowboy is a brewer—a very common combination; he uses the money of the depositors in carrying on the business of his brewery; and he does this the more easily if Mr. Safe be a partner in this concern.

also. This is a deviation from the principles laid down in the first place; for no one will contend that it is the same thing for the depositor to have his property dependent on the national credit, and to have it contingent on the credit and solvency of two gentlemen, however wealthy and upright, concerned in the manufacture of beer. However, if the brewery be carried on well and prudently, it may be safe enough; and the partners, aware of their ability to meet all demands made upon them, may be held excusable for strengthening one of their trades by means of the other. They are, nevertheless, under a comparative disadvantage in case of a panic; and their example might be pleaded and followed by Messrs. Slap, Dash, Hazard, and Crasher, who have joined half-a-dozen new and untried modes of business to their original one of bankers. We proceed, then, to the third step, that of hazardous business. And to this, and to what may be denominated over-trading, we attribute the fall of so many banking establishments. But here it will at once be evident that business which is perfectly safe and legitimate for a merchant or a financial company, may be in the highest degree unsafe for a banker. His securities must be not only good, but easily realizable; they may be wanted in the form of cash at a very short notice. And at this point it is that the actual history of banking commences. The Jews were the first who had the honour of being called bankers; but in the sense of the word which has been explained above they had small right to the appellation. They were pawnbrokers and money-lenders, as were the Lombards, who came after them. Then the goldsmiths took the business, and added the keeping of money and the receiving of rents, and other sources of income, and subsequently the circulation of notes, which were called goldsmiths' notes, and which took the place of our present bank-notes. As years rolled on, the trades of the goldsmith and the pawnbroker became dissevered from that of the banker, while those of the money-lender on land and monetary securities remained. Among these securities, bills of exchange soon formed an important item, and thus the banker became a bill discounter. Indeed, very high authorities have declared that the only legitimate use to which he can put the money confided to his care is by thus employing it.

From our very brief sketch of the theory and practice of banking, it is evident that so far as the element of risk can be eliminated out of any business, it should be from that of a banker especially. If he be a man of business, having a knowledge of business men, of the state of the money-market, and of the doctrines of monetary science, he can scarcely go very far wrong.

But the query is not yet fully answered: What business has a bank to break? They do break, and we have to tell the querist why. It is simply from neglect of the most ordinary precautions, from violation of the most universally recognised rules. What, for instance, can be more distinct, nay, more incompatible than the business of a banking and that of a finance company? The latter professes to supply money for great undertakings, such as would be impossible for individuals, and which do not in most cases offer a rapid return. They depend for their success on the development of a country's resources, on the prosperity of a town not yet built, on the return from mines not yet worked. These are legitimate objects for a finance company, but it is self-evident that they are not securities on which money should be advanced by a bank. They may be infinitely more profitable, but they are out of the proper line. They take too much time to fructify. The new town, such as that now building at Marseilles, may be a most lucrative speculation, but for their profits the speculators must wait till the houses are built and the rents come in, and for this again, they must wait till the additional commerce expected has developed itself. A railway across a chain of mountains may create a trade which shall abundantly repay the shareholders; but before they can expect a dividend from such a source, the source itself has to be called into existence. Such properties are extremely valuable, if they have time to ripen; but if in an undeveloped state a sale of shares be forced the losses must be enormous.

Let us then imagine—unfortunately no mere imaginary case—a bank either advancing large sums on such security, or what is the same thing, aiding a finance company so engaged. A period of panic comes, a "run" takes place on the bank, the shares of the inchoate undertaking are unsaleable, they fall to a heavy discount, are given away, money is even paid to those who will take them gratuitously; the bank is obliged to close its doors; a most useful work is brought to a dead stop, hundreds of families are ruined, and a good business destroyed, simply because the great fact has been lost sight of, that a banker's securities must be such, and only such, as can be readily turned into cash. But again, the very deposits which are particularly suited for the banker are in the highest degree unfitted for a finance company. Deposits of money to be paid on demand, or at short notice, are for such companies an abundant element of peril. Let there be a rumour, no matter how incorrect, that the town, the mine, the railway, or the manufactory, is in an unsatisfactory state, forthwith the depositors rush to the offices of the company to claim their money; and if the company has been so imprudent—we might, without much exceeding the bounds of truth, say so unprincipled—as to receive many such deposits, its securities will be forced into the market, and the result will be a "winding-up of the concern." Deposits on call or at short notice should be made with bankers only, and these, on the other hand, should carefully abstain from such business as belongs to finance companies. The late panic showed that both these rules have been systematically neglected, and hence no small part of the disturbances which have convulsed the money market.

It is but a slight story, but it is, nevertheless, a significative illustration of the careless security into which the managers of banks have been lulled of late, that such a fraud as the following could have been perpetrated:—

"I heard," says the London correspondent of the *Manchester Examiner*, "the other day, rather a curious story of a fraud successfully practised upon a couple of banks just before the panic. A certain Mr. X. had a large sum of money at bank A., on deposit account. Taking the deposit receipt with him, he went to bank B., and said that, for reasons, he did not wish to draw the money out, but would like an advance to the extent of two-thirds of the amount. The manager of the bank, with what seems foolish facility, but which might not do so if I mentioned names, granted the advance. Off goes X. to bank A., says that he wants the money on the instant, has not got the deposit receipt, but will send it round immediately. Can he obtain the money? 'Certainly,' says the manager. The money is accordingly paid, and, at present, X. is *non est*, having got both his original deposit and the advance upon it, each running to five figures. You may ask, whether you are likely to hear of this little matter in a criminal court? To which I reply, that you are not, for the present at any rate. I don't suppose that I need even hint at the obvious reason."

The following attempt to ruin a country banker by compelling him to stop payment, was actually put into practice some years ago. It is marked by such diabolical wickedness that, although the principal actor has been removed by death, it should be recorded, if only to show to what a pitch the spirit of revenge will impel a human being:—

On the establishment of the —— Fire Insurance

Company, its founder was appointed manager; and after the Company had been a few years in existence the conduct of this person was such as to call forth some severe remarks from the directors, and especially the chairman, who was a banker in the town of ——; in short, to such an extent had his misconduct been carried, that it became absolutely necessary, in order to protect the interests of the body of shareholders, that he should be requested to resign, or he would be dismissed. The duty of conveying the decision of the board devolved upon the chairman, who, in conclusion, told him that, on a given day, he would call at the office, and receive from Mr. B——, the manager, the books, securities, and moneys belonging to the Company then in his possession.

Accordingly, on the day appointed, the chairman, with two directors, called at the office, where they found Mr. B—— and his son, a young man, with a brace of pistols, sitting on a box which contained the securities, &c., belonging to the Company.. The young man was ordered by his father to shoot the first person that molested or attempted to move him from his seat. This hostile reception, so unlooked-for and unusual, astonished the chairman and directors, who accordingly retired to decide upon what steps it would, under these extraordinary circumstances, be desirable to take. On their leaving the premises, the manager called in twelve men, and told them he wanted them to walk in procession to Messrs. ——, the bankers; and he would march at their head.

It is necessary here to state, that the funds belonging to the company in the hands of the manager he had, since the day he received notice of the termination of his appointment, been engaged in exchanging for the bankers' notes, by which means he had accumulated several thousand pounds. The notes so collected he had attached to large sheets of paper, and pasted them on twelve boards like placards: one he carried himself, with these words in large characters:—"Going to Messrs. ——'s bank to demand payment." Each man carried one, and they marched in single file to the bank. On entering the house he demanded instant payment in gold; the clerks were taken by surprise; they had not so much gold in the bank; but they said they could in a very little time collect from the neighbouring banks the requisite amount. But no; this would not suit the manager; it was just the answer he expected. He replied, "These notes are payable to bearer on demand; I now demand instant payment, or I shall proclaim your bank as having failed."

The clerks entreated a few hours' indulgence, but he was inexorable; he would not give a minute, and turning to his men he said, "Now, my boys, shoulder your placards!" at the same time taking from his pocket a printed paper, with which he had come provided, he pasted it over the one he carried himself, and again headed the procession. This second placard announced that "Messrs. —— had suspended their payments;" and in this manner he marched through the principal streets, to the utter amazement of the inhabitants, especially those who had transactions with the bank. The result was as might have been anticipated—the bank failed. The object of the manager of the assurance company had been gained; he surrendered his appointment and left the town.

The end of this man, although terrible, was not so bad as he deserved. He died, we have been told, in the Fleet Prison, placed there by the very son who had, perhaps unwillingly, aided him in his former wicked career.

Of the issue of notes, the business of discounting, and the employment of capital, we shall speak in subsequent chapters.

CHAPTER V.

THE BANK OF ENGLAND AND ITS CHARTER.

Origin and Objects of the Bank of England—Its Early Success—Suspension of Cash Payments—The Restriction Act—Lord Stanhope's Act—Peel's Act of 1819—Ditto 1844—Convertible and Inconvertible Currency.

THE establishment of the Bank of England marks one of the most important periods in the monetary history of this country. It was, in the first place, a political act, and its object was to furnish the then sovereign, William III., with money to carry on those wars in which he was engaged. The plan adopted was that of William Paterson, and it provided that, by an Act granting to their majesties (William and Mary) several duties on the tonnage of ships and vessels, and upon ale, beer, and other liquors, certain recompenses should be made to such persons as should voluntarily advance the sum of fifteen hundred thousand pounds for carrying on the war with France. This sum was to be raised by subscription, and the subscribers were to form a corporation, and to be called "The Governor and Company of the Bank of England." This whole capital was to be paid over to Government, which was to pay £96,000 per annum as interest, and £4000 for management. The new corporation obtained a charter, which entitled it to borrow and lend—not to deal in merchandise, except to sell that on which money had been borrowed, and not repaid—but to traffic in bills of exchange and bullion. The plan was popular, the list of subscribers was filled in ten days, and on the 1st of January in the follow-year the new corporation issued its prospectus, and announced itself ready to issue notes, and to transact all other business. The restriction on the privilege of the Bank is exhibited by a clause prohibiting it from borrowing or owing more than the amount of its capital, and by making the individual members of the corporation liable to the creditors in proportion to the amount of their stock, if any such over-issue or over-borrowing took place. This charter was to be valid till 1705; it was then extended to 1710; and from that period it has been renewed from time to time till the present day. The stock of the company was exempted from all rates, taxes, assessments, or impositions of any kind whatsoever; and forgery of its notes, bills, and seal was declared felony. It was in addition to all these privileges enacted, that the corporation should continue in the enjoyment of this charter till the debt which the public had thus contracted with the Bank should be paid off. This charter bears date July 27th, 1694.

In the year 1708, an Act was passed prohibiting the formation of any other similar corporation; many such had been proposed by the Tories, for the Bank was a Whig project, and had been eminently successful in supporting the leaders of the party in the prosecution of the war. This, as it had excited the warmest feelings of joy and congratulation among the friends of the party, had also created bitter rage and indignation among their political enemies. Defeated in their endeavours to establish a rival corporation, they abandoned the design, and it has never been seriously entertained since. From that period the Bank has gone on lending the Government, at various periods, large sums of money, until in the year 1816 the debt to the Bank from the Government amounted to nearly twelve million pounds sterling. In the course of its progress the Bank became the Government agent in paying all dividends on account of the National Debt, and, generally speaking, managing all concerns connected with it. It will be unnecessary to pursue more minutely in this place the annals of this great corporation until we arrive at the year 1797. Three years previously to this the Bank had issued five-pound notes. In the year 1797 a panic occurred, and a great run upon the Bank took place. It was apprehended that great mischief would occur if a drain of bullion were occasioned by this; and an Order in Council appeared, prohibiting for a temporary period the payment of bank-notes in gold. This suspension of cash payments was sanctioned by public opinion; and important meetings were held to express confidence both in the Government and the Bank. On May 3, in the same year, the celebrated Bank Restriction Act passed; this confirmed and regulated the Order in Council, and the restriction was continued from time to time till the year 1819. During this long period the country passed through several monetary crises. The circulating medium had become deplorably deficient; it became necessary in 1777 to prohibit country bankers from issuing notes under £5, but this Act had to be repealed in 1798; and country bankers issued vast quantities of one-pound notes. The silver currency was wholly insufficient for the requirements of commerce; and the Bank took upon it the office of the Mint, and recoined a large issue of Spanish dollars, besides silver tokens of various values, for England and Ireland. The copper coinage was in an equally unsatisfactory state, not a tenth part of the currency was legitimate, and every town and a great number of private persons struck their own pennies, halfpennies, and farthings. In 1797, a new copper coinage appeared, and another in 1805-6; but the Royal Mint coined no silver till 1816—a piece of neglect on the part of the Government for which it is difficult to find any excuse. In fact, at this period of our history the nation was in a decidedly unprosperous condition: the national debt was increasing, prices were rising, and at the same time the working-classes were in a state of great distress and chronic discontent.

In the year 1810, the mischief seemed to have reached its height, and the Government were called upon to consider what share in the public distress was to be attributed to the continued suspension at the Bank of cash payments. A commission was appointed, but while it was admitted that an early return to cash payments was desirable, the Parliament did not act upon the recommendations of this report; and soon afterwards an attempt was made to force the reception of bank-notes as equal to gold in all payments whatsoever. This attempt is usually known as

Earl Stanhope's Act, because the bill was brought into Parliament by that nobleman. He had accepted Mr. Vansittart's theory, that bank-notes had not depreciated in value, but that gold had advanced, a fallacy which has lately been greatly current in America. Holding this notion, he proposed to make it a misdemeanour to take gold coin at more, or bank-notes for less, than their nominal value. The Act is said to have been determined on in consequence of a notice issued by Lord King to his tenants, and which we give entire, as exhibiting the mode of argument adopted at the time :—

"By lease, dated 1802, you have contracted to pay the annual rent of £47 5s. in good and lawful money of Great Britain. In consequence of the late great depreciation of paper-money, I can no longer accept any bank-notes at their nominal value in payment or satisfaction of an old contract. I must therefore desire you to provide for the payment of your rent in the legal gold coin of the realm; at the same time, having no other object than to secure payment of the real intrinsic value of the same, stipulated by agreement, and being desirous to avoid giving you any unnecessary trouble, I shall be willing to receive payment in either of the manners following, according to your option:—By payment in guineas; 2nd, if guineas cannot be procured, by a payment in Portugal gold coin, equal in weight to the number of guineas requisite to discharge the rent; 3rd, by a payment in bank-paper of a sum sufficient to purchase (at the present market price) the weight of standard gold requisite to discharge the rent. The alteration in the value of paper-money is estimated in this manner: the price of gold in 1802, the year of your agreement, was £4 an ounce; the present market price is £4 14*s.*, arising from the diminished value of paper. In that proportion an addition of £17 10*s.* per cent. in paper-money will be required as the equivalent for the payment of rent in paper."

This Bill passed, and was re-enacted from time to time along with the Bank Restriction Act.

But the time was now approaching when both these Acts were to fall together. In 1817 the Bank announced its intention of paying all its notes in gold, and it was stated in Parliament that more than five millions had been paid away in gold and taken to the Continent. The consequence of this was a new and stringent prohibition, which however lasted but a short time. In 1819, Sir Robert, then Mr. Peel, brought in his Bill for a return to cash payments. This was done gradually, and by May,

1823, the change was completely effected. At the same time all the laws which prohibited melting or exporting the coin were repealed. Another change took place at the same time, the expediency of which was more doubtful: the one and two-pound notes were withdrawn from circulation, no bank note after this time being for a less value than £5, and a large issue of sovereigns took place, the guinea being discontinued since 1816, as a coin inconvenient, because not in accordance with the monetary system of the country. Thus matters remained till 1824.

For some time past the interest on Government securities had been gradually diminished, and it was evidently the intention, and as evidently within the power of Government, to reduce that interest still further. This and other causes induced the public to look favourably on a multitude of joint-stock companies which were started at this critical period; so numerous were they, and on so great a scale, that had they been carried into effect they would have absorbed a capital of nearly £400,000,000 sterling! The year 1825 was marked by one of the most tremendous panics the mercantile world had ever experienced. The Bank had been compelled, in consequence of the adverse character of the foreign exchanges, to restrict its issues. This, and the damage done by the bubble companies of the preceding year, had produced a general state of unsoundness in the money market, and when, in the month of December, the banking-house of Sir Peter Pole and Co. stopped payment—a house of very high character, and connected with a host of country bankers—the impulse was given, and the panic soon declared itself in an aggravated form. It happened by a mere chance that a box of one-pound notes had been overlooked; these were at once issued by the Bank at a critical moment, and the panic slowly subsided.

Acts for renewing the charter passed in 1833 and in 1844, and in this last year that most important enactment, commonly called "Peel's Act." This Act regulated the issues of the Bank and of country bankers, and ascertained the amount of circulation in each case; it prohibited any increase of circulation, required each bank to publish at short intervals an account of its circulation in the *Gazette*, and where any increase appeared the bankers were compelled to hold coin or bullion to the amount of the excess. The Bank of England was permitted to issue notes to the amount of fourteen millions, that being the amount in which the Government stands indebted to the corporation. It further permits an issue of bank post-bills, for the convenience of remitters, to the extent of two millions. Beyond this no notes were to be issued that exceeded, even by five pounds, the actual bullion in the vaults of the Bank. The other clauses of this Act are of minor consequence.

From this brief sketch of the history and proceedings of the Bank, it will be manifest that it has complicated duties to perform, and that it is at once a bank of issue, a bank of deposit, the manager of the national debt, and the general regulator of exchanges. Now, at a period like the present, when the question is largely discussed whether the charter of the Bank should be renewed as it is, or whether, if renewed at all, it should not be with considerable modifications, it is well that the general public should be a little better informed than it is on the first principles of monetary science, and be, at all events, acquainted with the opinions of the best-informed men on these momentous subjects. As to the *importance* of the Bank to the nation there can be no doubt, and in the general opinion scarcely less that its action has been of the most advantageous character, and has tended not only to facilitate all monetary transactions, but to keep up the national credit at that point from which it has never fallen; but with regard to modifications in the charter there is a great variety of opinion, especially on the topic of a convertible or non-convertible currency of paper. The object of Sir Robert Peel's Act of 1844 was, *so far as possible,* to secure the former; but he evidently considered that this desideratum could not be absolutely secured, and regarded his own measure as of an elastic character. Indeed, when urged very strongly to relax the stringency of his plan, and convinced that times might come in which such relaxation would be necessary, he replied that "there would always be the alternative of an appeal to the Queen in Council."

The Bill assumed, as a principle, *that the amount of notes in circulation should rise or fall with the amount of bullion in the vaults of the bank which issued them.* But this is not a self-evident truth; if it be a truth at all, it is one which must be established by experience; and the experience necessary for this purpose requires many years for its attainment. It has an appearance of safety about it, looks like a renunciation of hazardous speculation, but is certainly contrary to the general analogy of mercantile transactions. No private banker, unless compelled by law, would confine his issues by any such proportions; and so satisfied have been bankers, governments, and the public in general, that the restriction is excessive, that it has never been fairly tried. In every period of panic the law has been at once relaxed. It was so in 1847, and since that, whenever the pressure has been such as to threaten danger. But a principle which its authors are willing to yield whenever hard pressed, cannot be one on which they have much dependence. It has never yet been acted upon—and if the experiment be ever tried at all, there seem grave doubts whether the present be the proper season for making it. The claims of the Bank itself ought to be considered. Its operations are greatly, and as many think, needlessly limited by the restrictions of this Act, while, on the other hand, the advantages conferred on the commercial world by the Bank are as generally admitted, and the very peculiar position of that corporation at the present time ought to have a liberal consideration.

Most people have heard of the "dead weight," but comparatively few know what it is. In the year 1823, just after the return to cash payments, Government had occasion for a large sum of money, in order to pension the retired officers of the army and navy and the widows of those who fell at Waterloo. To accomplish this, the ministry applied to the Bank, and covenanted that for and in consideration of £13,089,419, to be paid in the space of five years, they would pay to the Bank an annuity of £585,740 for the term of forty-four years. This annuity terminates, therefore, in the year 1867. This large sum will have to be deducted from the Bank's resources, and it will then be seen what amount of difficulty will be brought upon the corporation, and how far it is prepared for its altered income.

It is true that the whole of the transaction was to be condemned; it was contrary to all sound principles, and on one occasion, at least, it very nearly brought the Bank to a stoppage. The money was advanced out of the deposits made by the customers of the Bank, deposits payable on demand, and was, consequently, far too large a sum to be placed in this jeopardy. It was advanced in direct opposition to the terms of the Charter, which confine the operations of the corporation to dealing in bills of exchange and the buying and selling of bullion, and which strictly prohibit Bank directors from speculating in the funds. This was a purchase of a Government annuity, and the absolute transfer of a large sum of money deposited at call. So mischievous was the result of this unhappy purchase, that in 1839 the Bank was obliged to pledge a portion of the annuity to the East India

Company for the sum of £750,000, and this aid not proving sufficient, to borrow from foreign bankers the further sum of £2,500,000. A transaction was accomplished by means of accommodation-bills, drawn by Messrs. Baring and Co. on their correspondents in Paris, Hamburgh, and Amsterdam. In the month of September, 1839, the amount of gold in the coffers of the Bank was reduced to £2,727,000, while the circulation of notes was £17,906,000, and the Bank was liable for deposits at call to the extent of £7,600,000. Sir Robert Peel made use of this frightfully perilous state of affairs, when he proposed the measure which passed in 1844. That measure was a reaction, and probably went as far beyond the absolute requirements of the country as the state of preparation on the part of the Bank in 1839 fell short of them.

The question which has to be discussed may be thus expressed—Is it advisable that the restrictions placed on the Bank by the Act of 1844 be continued or removed? On the one hand are to be considered the claims of the Bank to the gratitude of the nation, as well as the policy of removing restrictions which have never been insisted on, when the occasion presented itself of testing their efficacy. On the other hand, the danger of taking a step towards an inconvertible currency. No one doubts that the pecuniary difficulties of Austria have to a large extent arisen from an unlimited indulgence in this fascinating, but most perilous nostrum. We have yet to see how far the greater resources and more energetic character of the American people will enable them to bear up under its pressure. The theory of such a currency is easy enough, and the facts have always as yet been in accordance with it. We cannot wonder that any measure, however partial, which tends towards the re-establishment of so unsound a principle, should be looked on with jealous watchfulness, and especially when such vast mischief has been effected by panic manufacturers, whose unhallowed occupation has grown into a system, and bids fair to become more and more productive of commercial distress.

The man who knows that he cannot get his five-pound note changed at the Bank to-day, but that the cause is a temporary "tightness" in the money market, and that to-morrow, the pressure being removed, he shall have no difficulty in the matter, will easily find persons willing to give him five sovereigns for his note, and it will pass on without question or hesitation. No effect on prices was produced by the removal of bank restrictions in 1847, nor has the suspension of the Act ever had any such effect. Again, the same agencies which can check a panic may by a parity of reason be relied on, if applied in time to prevent it. If it were known that in cases of emergency the powers of the Bank will be set at liberty, that houses of good standing and sound character may rely on assistance, and that the Bank issues will be enlarged for that purpose, "operators for the fall" would in many cases abstain from their "operations," and in all would have to restrict within far narrower bounds their work of disturbing credit. Perhaps, while keeping to the present practice of imposing restrictions on the amount of issue, and relaxing them when necessary, it might be worth while simply to enlarge the amount permitted, and make it more nearly approximate that which a safe theory of banking would recognise. This, with a gradual increase in the issues of branch banks, and an equally gradual withdrawal from circulation of the notes issued by country bankers, might meet all the exigencies of the case. One thing is certain, that a panic under existing circumstances is an extremely dangerous thing, and it is like the cholera, or any other epidemic, not to be waited for before we take measures against it. Our commercial measures should be precautionary. Panics will be more frequent when their promoters find that they can be made the means of profit, and we should have our chloride of lime ready for the first miasmata that make their appearance.

These are valid reasons for not hastily removing restrictions, which, as we have seen, need never be allowed to stand in the way when a necessity occurs for enlarged action. Against these may be adduced the arguments already cited. There is an immense difference between an inconvertible paper currency and a partially convertible one. The one brings down the value of money and raises the price of commodities, affects the credit of the nation, and is invariably followed by a reaction, often terribly destructive. The other seems to have none of these frightful results.

CHAPTER VI.

NATIONAL DEBTS OR OBLIGATIONS—ENGLISH AND FOREIGN.

How National Debts arose—Illustrated by Examples—Questions to be Solved—National and Governmental Obligations—Case of Prussia—Case of Virginia—Case of Greece—Supposed Beneficial Effect of a National Debt—the Case Examined.

IN the coming chapters of this work, I shall have frequent occasion to speak of the Funds, the National Debt, the public creditor, the rise and fall of various descriptions of Stock, and the multifarious operations of the Stock Exchange.

To make this intelligible we must ascertain what all these terms mean, and treat somewhat extensively on the manner in which nations contract debts, and the modes which they adopt in liquidating them. The *rationale* of such proceedings does not differ from that of ordinary contracts between individuals, and they are of course governed by the same laws of mercantile morality; for that which is morally wrong cannot be politically right, and a swindle does not cease to be a swindle because it is endorsed by a minister of state, nor even because the will of a whole nation has concurred in its perpetration. But inasmuch as there are certain differences between the manner in which the individual gets into debt, and that in which the nation does so, I will just state in the plainest way possible the position of the state and the fundholder respectively at the present time, and with regard to our own country. There is a great debt which is called the National Debt. Is it a heavy weight about the neck of the people? or is it rather, as many think, an advantage?—ought it ever to have been contracted? These points will be brought out in the discussion of the following questions :—

Who is the public creditor?

What is the nature of his claim?

Is it, or is it not, founded in strict justice?

Is there any probability of its liquidation?

National debts, our own among the number, are contracted in the manner following :—

Some cause requiring larger expenditure than usual, generally war, renders the income of a government inadequate to its requirements, and that to so great an extent that additional taxes cannot be imposed to meet the urgency of the case. Under these circumstances, the Government negotiates a loan—the State borrows money precisely in the same way as any private individual would, offering that rate of interest requisite to insure the obtaining the needful sum, and giving the creditor security on the public revenue.

The sum thus borrowed, and for which interest is paid, is usually called the "Funds," or "Government Securities," neither of which terms are precisely applicable; for the money itself does not exist, and the securities bear the same relation to that for which they are "securities," as do other documents bearing the same name.

The national debt of this country amounts to nearly £800,000,000 sterling. A large part of this enormous sum was expended in the struggle with France under Napoleon, the result of which was the destruction of the French Empire, the restoration of the French Royalty, and the settlement of Europe upon what were then called legitimate principles. Not far short of fifty millions was expended in the Crimean war, previous to which the debt had been greatly reduced during the long peace.

Whatever opinions may be held now concerning those events, I think it can hardly be denied that they were at the time absolutely necessary to the safety of this country, and that they were carried on in conformity with the public will, if not in direct obedience to it. The act was therefore a national act as contradistinguished from an act of the Government.

The persons who at any period of our history have for public purposes advanced money to the Government, or, if it be thought a better mode of expression, have invested money in Government Securities, *were* the public creditors; those on whom by purchase or descent their claims have devolved, *are* so at the present time.

The justice of the claim made and allowed at this time must depend on the joint conduct of the debtor and creditor; and in order to get at this, we must examine the way in which the debt has increased or diminished, and the faith which has been kept in matter of interest to the creditor.

It will be seen that the claim itself is one of very simple character. A says, "My father lent the Government, in his day, £10,000, for which he covenanted to receive 5 per cent. interest; he bequeathed that claim to me, and it has been allowed; but I am only receiving $3\frac{1}{2}$ per cent. for the same." But, on further inquiry, we shall find that at a particular period the Government stated to A's father, and to all who were in his position— "The value of money is less now than it was when we borrowed it from you; we shall, therefore, only pay 4 instead of 5 per cent.; but as we are bound by our contract with you, we propose to you either to continue your loan to us on this reduced interest, or to receive back the sum originally paid, and this we will effect by a new loan." A's father accepted the first of the two alternatives; and, by a subsequent reduction made in the same way, he found his interest brought down to $3\frac{1}{2}$ per cent., at which rate an income is now paid to A. Nothing can be fairer than this; some portions of the debt have been paid off, and it is at present rather diminishing than increasing.

But some persons, who fancy that the abolition of the debt would place England in a higher position than that which she at present occupies, have endeavoured to persuade themselves and others that the claim of the fundholder is not founded in justice; and their arguments take the following form:—"The money borrowed was borrowed for the defence of the nation, but as the nation was bound to defend itself, the money ought not to have been *lent*, but *given*; and as the *property* of the nation was what was in danger, so the defence of it was the especial duty of those who possessed that property; *i.e., the rich*, or, in other words, those who advanced the money in question." The inference from this curiously fallacious argument is, that we have been wrong in paying any interest at all, and shall be still more wrong if we continue to pay it. It amounts, in fact, to this, that A, the nation, borrowed from B, the individual, money to pay B's debts; that, having done this, A pays B a perpetual interest for the money so borrowed. Whereas B ought to have paid the debt, or liquidated the obligation himself, and so terminated the matter.

All this supposes—1. That property was the only thing at stake—the keeping of our national freedom, the preservation of our old laws and religion, our commercial independence, and our colonial empire—all being entirely overlooked, or regarded only as interesting to the comparatively small body of fundholders. 2. It entirely misstates the case; if the money were borrowed for *national* purposes, the *nation* was bound to repay it, or at least to pay the stipulated interest; and the fundholders, as a portion of the nation, pay a portion of the taxes, whereby their own claim is satisfied. Thus, as it was the nation which borrowed, so it is the nation which pays. The case may be rendered still clearer by an illustration: A community of thirty persons have need, for their common use, of a sum of thirty thousand pounds—*i.e.*, they want one thousand pounds each. The natural solution of the question is, that each should pay the sum of one thousand pounds, and the common interest be consulted by the common sacrifice.

But when the proposition is made, it is found that twenty-eight out of the thirty are not in a condition to furnish their quota. The business or enterprise in which they are engaged is prosperous, and will well reward them for this necessary outlay; but though the share of each in it is worth much more than a thousand pounds, only two of the thirty are able to furnish the sum of money.

Under these circumstances, the two rich members say, "We will advance fifteen thousand pounds each; but as we are not legally bound to advance more than the fifteenth part of that sum, and our money is worth to us 5 per cent., so the community—*i.e.*, the thirty persons—must tax themselves to furnish the fifteen hundred pounds which will be annually required for interest. In that taxation we, the advancers of the whole sum, thus take our part, all interests are consulted, the credit of the community saved, and a species of mutual assurance is effected."

This is the exact case with the nation at large and the national creditor.

From this it will appear that the application of

the sponge to the National Debt—a favourite nostrum of some political quacks—or the applying the annual interest to liquidate the principal, either of which would constitute an act of national bankruptcy, can be justified only by the same circumstances which justify any private bankruptcy—viz., the ascertained inability to pay either principal or interest.

A national debt contracted under such circumstances as ours was has a double amount of obligation, for it was not only contracted for national objects, but by the clearly and unmistakably expressed will of the nation itself. A debt might be contracted by the Government of Prussia, for example, to carry on a war with Austria to annex Holstein and Schleswig, and finally to take possession of the rest of Denmark, and this might be called a *national* debt, but as it would be one the objects of which would, in their own nature, be unjust and immoral, and would not command the sympathies of the people, a question might arise whether the payment of such a debt would be morally obligatory on any but the government which contracted it. Policy, however, would probably dictate its acknowledgment—at least in Europe; but supposing such a war to be successfully carried out, and the countries named to be annexed to the Prussian monarchy, it would then be competent to the victors to throw the whole weight of the debt on the vanquished, nor would there be any way open of escaping this oppression save by revolt or foreign interference. Similar cases have occurred, and they tend to show that many obligations are called national, and treated as such, when they were in fact only governmental. A very remarkable instance has just been exhibited in America. In their resistance to the demands of the North, the Southern states of the great Republic incurred heavy debts, each state on its own responsibility. After the conclusion of the war the victorious party required the repudiation of all these debts as a condition for being permitted again to enter the Union.

According to all rules, alike of mercantile or political morality, this was to compel an act of dishonesty. If Virginia, on the security of her own state resources, purchased from Liege a thousand muskets, the fact that Virginia was worsted in the contest furnishes no argument against the duty of paying for the arms. It might have been competent for Virginia to say, " I am wasted and desolate, my strife has been in vain, my homes are devastated, my resources cut short, and my prospects blighted—I cannot pay." Had she pleaded thus, all that could have been said in reply might be summed up in the words, "The more's the pity." But she did not plead thus; she would willingly have paid; but the victorious North prohibited this honest and honourable course, and again sanctioned, by the declaration of the national will, the policy of repudiation.

In our case there is no ground for such a proceeding, and, happily for the character of the British people, no desire to recur to it.

Many foreign debts, and notably those of the South American republics, have been contracted in order to achieve their political independence. That of Greece arose in the same way; and some others have been incurred to carry on works of general utility—to build and adorn cities, to make canals and aqueducts, to construct harbours, and to aid in various ways the real interests of the nations who have contracted them. The mode in which such debts are contracted is usually somewhat as follows: The Government, desirous of obtaining a loan, applies to a great capitalist, and proposes to him the negotiation. Let us suppose that the Government is that of Chili, and the House of Baring be selected for the business. The amount required is stated, and the revenues of the Customs at Valparaiso are hypothecated to pay the interest, and in due time to liquidate the principal. One million sterling is wanted, and the interest offered is 6 per cent.; but no capitalist will invest on such terms, so he is not asked to pay his hundred pounds, but some smaller sum, say seventy pounds. With that seventy pounds he purchases an obligation from the Chilian Government to pay him £100 in a stipulated time, and in the meanwhile to pay him six pounds for every seventy so advanced. Messrs. Baring examine the proposal. They introduce the loan to the notice of European capitalists, and the money is raised.

Now let us look at the position of the holder of this stock. He has paid seventy per cent., and his bonds are to bear interest at six. Suppose him to have purchased them to the extent of £700 sterling, he will have £1000 in the stock and sixty pounds per annum; thus he will receive between $8\frac{1}{2}$ and 9 per cent. for his money, and his security will be that the Customs receipts at Valparaiso are covenanted to be devoted to that purpose.

It is unnecessary to say that among foreign debts are found every variety of security, rendering some quite as safe as our own, and stamping others as among the most transparent of impositions. On this subject more will be said in the chapters on the Stock Exchange. I conclude this chapter with a few observations on the much-mooted question, Is the national debt an advantage to the nation or otherwise? At first sight this would seem to be scarcely deserving of a moment's consideration, for why should a heavy debt, which consumes nearly a third of a nation's income in paying interest upon it, be a benefit to a nation, any more than a similar incumbrance would be to a private individual? However, the theory is still held by so many, that it is worth investigating. It is said, then—

First, that the existence of the debt binds the people to the Government, for if that were overthrown the debt would go with it, and the fundholders would lose their money.

Secondly, that it affords a safe and moderate investment, giving therefore an opportunity for many thousands of persons with small properties of living on their incomes with quiet and security.

Thirdly, that its existence is a warning to Government not to engage in rash wars or extravagant expences.

Fourthly, that it creates a vast amount of business, and thus furnishes employment for many thousand persons.

I do not recollect any other arguments in favour of a national debt, and it is not difficult to refute all these, and to show that a state of indebtedness is as much an evil to a nation as it is to an individual. It may be an unavoidable evil, but can hardly, except by a curious perversion of language, be called an advantage. For, taking in order the benefits which it is supposed to produce, we may remark—

First, that the fundholders form a very small minority of the people, and that it is not simply by *their* allegiance that the Government is upheld.

Secondly, that there has never been any serious want of loyalty among the people of this country, and there always has been a great amount of moral rectitude. A Government which was capable of so far trampling upon the rights of property as to repudiate the national debt would have no chance of acceptance with a right-loving and law-abiding people; and if, on the other hand, the mere material interests, as understood by themselves, of the great masses were consulted, it is clear that they would prefer a state of affairs which would reduce rather than one which would continue a heavy system of taxation. From these considerations it is clear that the existence of an enormous national debt does not bind the people to the Government.

Thirdly, if the national debt were paid off to-morrow, though there would be a great difficulty for a while in finding investments for persons of small property, yet before long capital would find openings for employment, and affairs would go on with their accustomed regularity.

Fourthly, it may be very gravely doubted whether the supposed effect is produced at all. Most thinking people agree in the need of great retrenchment in the expences of our own Government, and it has never appeared that the fear of adding to our fiscal burdens has had much efficacy in this direction.

Fifthly, it may be admitted that thousands of persons are employed in various ways connected with the national debt, and that its abolition would entail their dismissal; but on this ground we might proclaim a pestilence to be a benefit, because it employed a great number of physicians.

At the same time we may see that the results have not been *all* evil. There have been periods in our history when the existence of the debt *has* tended to confirm the wavering. It does afford a safe investment for moderate fortunes, and it does furnish employment to many thousand persons. It is probable that the vast increase in the national debt of France has been deliberately encouraged by the sagacity of the present Emperor, with a view of binding the French people to his own dynasty. It is far more likely to have that effect in France than among ourselves, for the French funds are divided among a much larger number of holders, and so far as the desired result is obtained, so far must it be for the benefit of France and of the world at large. A revolution in that country must always produce a wide-spread disturbance elsewhere.

CHAPTER VII.

PUBLIC FUNDS—CONSOLS—EXCHEQUER BILLS, ETC.

The Funds—Consols—Other Government Stock—The Unfunded Debt—Mediæval Loans—Revenue Anticipated—Irredeemable Debt—Acts of Consolidation—Perpetual Annuities—Dr. Price's opinions—Variations in the Price of Stocks—Causes of such Variation.

FROM the Philosophy of National Debts we come to the Practice. Our own debt presents itself to our view in the form of various funds, bearing interest, and serving as investments to many thousands of persons. Taking them in something like the order of their importance, we have—

I. CONSOLS.—This word is an abbreviation of Three per Cent. Consolidated Bank Annuities. It forms by far the greater part of the public debt. It had its origin in 1751, when an Act was passed consolidating several separate stocks bearing an interest of three per cent. The present amount of this stock is about £400,000,000.

The interest upon it has never failed, and as it forms the favourite investment of the nation, it is supposed to be especially affected by all that affects the national interest.

II. REDUCED THREES.—This word is used to imply reduced Three per Cent. Annuities. The stock commenced in 1757. It consisted, as the name implies, of stocks which had borne previously a higher rate of interest, and whose holders had the option afforded them of being paid off or accepting the lower rate. Most of them chose the latter alternative. It amounts at present to about £110,000,000.

III. NEW THREES, which till October, 1854, paid $3\frac{1}{4}$ per cent., having previously undergone several conversions from their original denomination as "Navy Five per Cents." The present rate of interest is secured from further reduction till October, 1874, and dividends are payable April 5th and October 10th. The amount of this stock is £246,245,910.

IV. NEW FIVES, comprising the residue of the Navy Five per Cents., but amounting altogether to a comparatively insignificant sum. They are secured from reduction till after January, 1875. Dividends payable January 5th and July 5th.

V. INDIAN FIVES, liable to being paid off at par, or the interest being reduced, in 1870.

LIFE ANNUITIES, which may be obtained from the Commissioners for the Reduction of the National Debt, at their office in the Old Jewry, in exchange for stock or money, on single or joint lives, calculated according to age, at fixed rates.

THE UNFUNDED DEBT consisted at one time wholly of Exchequer Bills.

These are bills of credit issued by authority of Parliament. They are for various sums, and bear interest (generally from $1\frac{1}{2}d.$ to $2\frac{1}{2}d.$ per diem per £100) according to the usual rate at the time. The advances of the Bank to Government are made upon Exchequer Bills, and the daily transactions between the Bank and Government are principally carried on through their intervention. Notice of the time at which outstanding Exchequer Bills are to be paid off is given by public advertisement. Bankers prefer investing in Exchequer Bills to any other species of stock, even though the interest be for the most part comparatively low, because the capital may be received at the Treasury at the rate originally paid for it, the holders being exempted from any risk of fluctuation. Exchequer Bills were first issued in 1696, and have been annually issued ever since.

EXCHEQUER BONDS are a similar description of securities to the last mentioned, except that the Bonds are not payable annually. They were introduced by Mr. Gladstone in 1853, as part of a scheme for the conversion of some portion of the permanent debt into a terminable one. In the course of the negotiation, however, circumstances arose to defeat the success of the measure, the result being that a very small amount of Bonds were taken up. In the following year, the South Sea Stock proprietors having claimed payment, and the prospect of a war against Russia having created a heavy demand on the Exchequer, the same Chancellor determined on renewing the attempt to create Exchequer Bonds, instead of resorting at once to a regular loan. Bonds were, therefore, advertised, bearing interest at the rate of 3½ per cent. per annum, payable half-yearly, in three sets of £2,000,000 each—the Bonds classed A, B, and C, to be payable May 8th, 1858; May 8th, 1859; and May, 1860; the Bonds to be issued in amounts of £100, £200, £500, and £1000. Of these Bonds, however, only Classes A and B were ever taken up—to the amount, it is understood, of nearly £4,000,000. The dividends thereon are payable in May and November. These are the chief Government securities.

The first attempt towards defraying the expenses of a war by regular loans was made by the State of Florence in the year 1341, when the Government, finding itself in debt to the amount of £60,000, and unable immediately to discharge the debt, formed the principal sum into an aggregate joint-stock divided into shares, which were made transferable, bearing interest at five per cent. per annum, and varying in price according to the state of public credit.

Though at so early a period as that we have mentioned, the system now generally adopted was understood in Italy and put in practice; yet it was not till the end of the seventeenth century that

Louis XIV. of France funded, as it is called, though in a very irregular manner, the debts incurred by him in his long and expensive wars.

For several years no other mode was thought of than that of anticipation; and parliamentary provision was invariably made for the liquidation of such debts by means of annuities of various kinds, and of taxes appropriated to particular debts, calculated to produce both interest and a surplus towards the discharge of the principal.

It was reserved for the Government of George I. to break through this salutary regulation, for we find that in the early part of his reign the doctrine of raising money by way of loan, and providing only for the payment of the interest, leaving the principal to be paid by posterity, was first adopted by the English Ministry, who finding it necessary to raise money, thought it safer to transfer the public debt to posterity than at that time to irritate the public mind by increasing the taxes for the discharge of the principal.

This policy gave rise to the Acts passed in the years 1715, 1716, and 1717, by which the several taxes appropriated to the discharge of the debts of the Government, were consolidated in four funds—viz., the Aggregate, the South Sea, the General, and the Sinking Fund. The latter was formed from the surplus of the three former, and was intended for the purpose of reducing, and ultimately discharging, the debts of the nation.

To each of these funds a variety of duties was appropriated, comprehending altogether the whole revenue, except the Land Tax and Malt Tax, which were granted annually, and other branches then appropriated to the support of the civil Government. This was the commencement of the funding system.

The Perpetual Annuities are distinguished according to the rate of interest they pay, or the time and purpose of their creation. When the Government, by a new loan, contracts an additional debt bearing a certain fixed rate of interest, it is usual to add the capital thus created to the amount of that part of the public debt which bears the same interest and name, and to add the produce of the taxes levied for the payment of the interest of such new debt to the fund provided for paying the interest of the original or former capital; thus consolidating the old and new debts, and making the whole interest payable out of the general produce of the same fund: hence we have the Three per Cent. Consolidated Annuities, &c. When the Government were desirous of borrowing money, the Three per Cents. were generally preferred; and supposing they could not negotiate a loan for less than 4½ per cent., the object was effected by giving the lender, in return for every £100 advanced, £150.

In consequence of the prevalence of this practice, the principal of the debt now existing amounts to nearly one-fifth more than the sum actually advanced by the lenders.

On this subject Dr. Price, in his preface to the third edition of his " Observations on Reversionary Annuities," p. 14, says—" Were a person in private life to borrow £100 at 5 per cent. on condition it should be reckoned £200 borrowed at 2½ per cent., he would, by subjecting himself to the necessity, if he ever discharged the debt, of paying double the sum he received, gain something of the air of borrowing at two-and-a-half per cent., though he really borrowed at five. But would such a person be thought in his proper senses? One cannot indeed, without pain, consider how needlessly the capital of our debts has been, in several instances, increased. Thus do spendthrifts go on, loading their estates with debts, careless what difficulties they throw on the discharge of the principal, leaving that to their successors, and satisfied with any expedients that will make things do their time."

The price of stocks is influenced by a variety of

VARIATIONS IN PRICE. 91

circumstances. Whatever tends to shake or increase the public confidence in the stability of Government, tends at the same time to lower or to raise the price of stocks. They are also affected by the state of the revenue; and more than all by the facility of obtaining supplies of disposable capital, and the interest which may be realized upon loans to responsible persons. From 1730 till the rebellion of 1745, the Three per Cents. were never under 80, and were once, in June, 1737, as high as 107. During the rebellion they sank to 76; but in 1749 rose again to 100. In the interval between the peace of Paris in 1763, and the breaking out of the American War, they averaged from 80 to 90; but towards the close of the war they sank to 54. In 1792, they were, at one time, as high as 96. In 1797, the prospects of the country, owing to the successes of the French, the mutiny in the fleet, and other adverse circumstances, were by no means favourable; and in consequence the price of the Three per Cents. sank, on the 20th of September, on the intelligence transpiring of an attempt to negotiate with the French Republic having failed, to $47\frac{3}{8}$, being the lowest price to which they had ever fallen.

A few words will be necessary on the subject of foreign loans; these will be considered chiefly as investments, the principle of loans having been sufficiently investigated in those chapters which treat of our own. None of these are equal in security to those of our own Government, and some are of a kind so especially "risky" as to make all prudent persons unwilling to meddle with them. Austria has paid her interest duly and fully, but her financial prospects on the eve of war are not promising, and her internal condition in a monetary point of view is the reverse of favourable. Belgian stock is safer, for even should Belgium lose her independence, she can only lose it to France, and France will pay all her obligations. Brazilian is good; the empire is rich and quiet, and too far from the United States to be much affected by that turbulent power. Buenos Ayres has behaved badly, but promises well for the future; moreover, she has the power to keep her promises. Chili is very safe; the commerce carried on is considerable, and the interest has for some time past been regularly paid. The Peruvian debt is secure for the present, that is, as long as the guano on the Chincha Islands lasts; after that is carried away, the debt will probably assume a less agreeable aspect. The other South American republics are careless of their reputation, and appear totally destitute of any moral sense. In Europe, Denmark, Holland,

and Sweden have always paid punctually the interest on their debt, as have Russia and Turkey, but there is a degree of uncertainty respecting the interior condition of both these empires, which renders their securities less valuable than those previously named.

These foreign debts pay their interest by means of coupons, a sheet of which is attached to each bond; the coupon itself being a small square division capable of being easily detached from the rest, and representing half-a-year's interest. These bonds with their coupons are transferable from hand to hand, they require no endorsement, and hence are more convenient as negotiable securities, and at the same time more liable to be stolen, and if lost, less likely to be recovered.

CHAPTER VIII.

OF THE STOCK EXCHANGE—BROKERS—JOBBERS, ETC.

History and Business of the Stock Exchange—Mode of Transfer—Brokers, Jobbers, and Speculators—Bulls, Bears, and Lame Ducks—Time Bargains—High Character of the Stock Exchange—Nature and Manner of Gambling—Tragedy of the Money Market.

As all other markets have their localities, so the money market, though carrying on its operations wherever the great agent of commerce is at work, has nevertheless its special place of action—its mart for securities—its locality for the meetings of bankers, merchants, brokers, jobbers, buyers and sellers of stocks and shares, and all who deal or speculate in money. In London, which may be called the financial metropolis of the world, this locality is about the centre of the City proper. It comprehends the Bank, the Royal Exchange, the Stock Exchange, most of the houses of the chief bankers, the joint-stock banks, the finance and discount companies, the great insurance offices, and nearly all the principal establishments connected with or dependent on these. A little farther to the east are the Corn and Coal Exchanges, and beyond these, still farther, in the same direction, lie the wine markets, the Docks, and all that constitutes London a port of the first magnitude. How little these limits are changed may be seen from the words of an old writer, who, nearly a century ago, discusses the same topic:—

"The centre of jobbing is in the kingdom of Change Alley and its adjacencies. The limits are easily surrounded in a minute and a half. Stepping out of Jonathan's into the Alley, you turn your face full south; moving on a few paces, and then turning due east, you advance to Garraway's; from thence, going out at the other door, you go on still east into Birchin Lane; and then, halting a little at the Sword Blade Bank, you immediately face to the north, enter Cornhill, visit two or three petty provinces there on your way to the west; and thus having boxed your compass, and sailed round the stock-jobbing globe, you turn into Jonathan's again."*

Arrangements for the sale of stock are generally made at the Stock Exchange (situated in Capel Court, opposite to the Bank), which is frequented by brokers, buyers, and sellers, and a body of inter-

* Jonathan's Coffee House served as a Stock Exchange about the year 1770.

mediate agents called *jobbers,* whose business is to accommodate the buyers and sellers of stock with the exact sums they want. A jobber is generally possessed of considerable property in the funds; and he declares a price at which he will either sell or buy. Thus, he declares he is ready to buy 3 per Cent. Consols at $85\frac{1}{2}$, or to sell at $85\frac{5}{8}$; so that, in this way, a person willing to buy or sell any sum, however small, has never any difficulty in finding an individual with whom to deal. The jobber's profit is generally $\frac{1}{8}$ per cent., for which he transacts both a sale and a purchase. He frequently confines himself entirely to this sort of business, and engages in no other description of stock speculation. The broker is a distinct person—he is simply the agent, who buys and sells for his principal.

That a stock-broker should be a man of good standing and character is evident, considering the magnitude and importance of the business which he has to transact. To secure this he should be a member of the Stock Exchange. This implies that he should have been regularly recommended to the Exchange by three members, who become at the same time security for him during a limited period. He then becomes a member, pays ten guineas per annum for the privilege, and as much for any clerk whom he may authorize to act in his name. His dealings are under the general supervision of his co-members—not far from a thousand in number—and any overt dishonourable conduct is invariably punished by expulsion. The Stock Exchange is governed, or rather managed, by a committee of thirty persons, and if any dispute arise between a broker and his client, it may be referred to this committee, who will investigate the question and arbitrate between the two. So various and so numerous are the checks upon irregularity, and so jealous is the Stock Exchange of its honour, that in all intelligent circles the character of a stockbroker is looked upon with great and well-merited respect.

The same may be unhesitatingly said also of the stock-jobber, if he be *a member* of the body in Capel Court. But there is a notion in many minds that the jobber is merely a speculator in stock—a kind of gambler, who lives by the profit he can make on his own ventures, and is often in no condition to pay his losses, should he incur any. This is an error. He is in reality a stock-merchant—he acts according to the best of his judgment in purchasing such stocks as he thinks will rise, and be therefore in demand; and he sells, like other men of business, when he expects a fall, and desires to limit his own losses. All respectable jobbers are members of the Stock Exchange, subject to its rules and sharing its reputation.

Those who have business to transact, unless it be on a large scale and they themselves professionals, are rarely brought into contact with the jobber at all. They apply to the broker, who obtains from the jobber the particular amount of the stock required, and effects its transfer to his principal. It is not considered *advisable* for a jobber to be a broker also; and though there are many who combine the two branches, they are looked upon with some distrust by the highest members of the profession. As a rule, it is expedient for persons unversed in the mysteries of the Stock Exchange, whenever they have business there, to employ a *sworn* broker—that is, who has obtained a licence from the City, and who confines himself strictly to buying and selling upon commission.

A bargain for the sale of stock being agreed on, it is carried into execution at the Transfer Office at the Bank, or the South Sea House. For this purpose the seller makes out a note in writing, which contains the name and designation of the seller and purchaser, and the sum and description of the stock to be transferred. He delivers this to the proper clerk* and then fills up a receipt—a printed form of which, with blanks, is obtained at the office. The clerk, in the meantime, examines the seller's accounts, and if he finds him possessed of the stock proposed to be sold, makes out the transfer. This is signed in the books by the seller, who delivers the receipt to the clerk; and upon the purchaser's signing his acceptance in the book, the clerk signs the receipt as a witness. It is then delivered to the purchaser upon payment of the money, and thus the affair is completed.

This business is generally transacted by the brokers, who derive their authority from their employers by powers of attorney. Forms of these are obtained at the respective offices. Some authorize the broker to sell, others to accept a purchase, and others to receive the dividends. Some comprehend all these objects, and the two last are generally united. Powers of attorney, authorizing to sell, must be deposited in the proper office for examination one day before selling; a stockholder acting personally, after granting a letter of attorney, revokes it by implication.

* The letters of the alphabet are placed round the room, and the seller must apply to the clerk who has his station under the initial of his name. In all the offices, there are supervising clerks, who join in witnessing the transfer.

The person in whose name the stock is invested when the books are shut, previous to the payment of the dividends, receives that for the half year preceding; and therefore, a purchaser during the currency of the half year has the benefit of the interest on the stock he buys, from the last term of payment to the day of transfer, unless a special reservation is made, in which case the stock is said to be sold *ex div.*—*i.e.*, without the dividend. The price of stock, therefore, rises gradually, *cæteris paribus*, from term to term ; and when the dividend is paid, it undergoes a fall equal thereto. Thus the 3 per Cent. Consols should be higher than the 3 per Cent. Reduced by $\frac{3}{4}$ per cent. from the 6th April to the 5th of July, and from the 10th of October to the 5th of January; and should be as much lower from the 5th of January to the 5th of March, and from the 5th of July to the 10th of October; and this is nearly the case. Accidental circumstances may occasion a slight deviation.

The dividends on the different stocks being payable at different terms, it is in the power of stockholders to invest their property in such a manner as to draw their income quarterly.

The business of speculating in the Stocks is founded on the variation of the price of stock, which variation it probably tends in some measure to perpetuate. It consists in buying and selling stock according to the views entertained by those who engage in this occupation, of the probability of stock rising or falling.

It is or should be conducted by persons who have property in the funds; but a practice also prevails among those who have no such property, of contracting for the sale of stock on a future day at a price agreed upon. For example, A may agree to sell to B £10,000 of 3 per Cent. Stock, to be transferred in twenty days for £6000. A has, in fact, no such stock; but if the price on the day appointed for the transfer be only 58, he may purchase as much as will enable him to fulfil his bargain for £5800, and thus gain £200 by the transaction; on the other hand, if the price of that stock should rise to 62, he will lose £200. The affair is generally settled without any actual purchase of stock or transfer, A paying to B, or receiving from him the difference between the price of the stock on the day of settlement and the price agreed upon. Bargains of this kind are called time bargains.

This practice, which amounts to nothing else than a wager concerning the price of stock, is not sanctioned by law, yet it is carried on to a great extent; and as neither party can be compelled by law to complete these bargains, their sense of honour, and the disgrace attending a breach of contract, form the principles by which the business is governed. In the language of the Stock Exchange, the buyer is called *a Bull*, the seller *a Bear*, and the person who refuses to pay his loss, a *Lame Duck*. The names of defaulters are exhibited on a large black board in the Stock Exchange, where they dare not appear afterwards.

These bargains are usually made for certain days fixed by a committee of the Stock Exchange, called *settling days*, of which there are about eight in the year—viz., one in each of the months of January, February, March, May, July, August, October, November; and they are always on Tuesday, Wednesday, Thursday, or Friday, being the days on which the Commissioners for the Reduction of the National Debt make purchases.

The settling days in January and July are always the first days of opening the Bank books for public transfer; and these are notified at the Bank when the Consols are shut to prepare for the dividend. The price at which stock is sold to be transferred on the next settling day, is called the *price on account*. Sometimes, instead of closing the account on the settling day, the stock is carried on to a future day, on such terms as the party agree on. This is called *a continuance*.

In the account of Stock Exchange transactions the terms "put and call," "options," "backwardation"—a most awkward and ill-contrived word, by-the-bye—are frequently met with. These have reference to time bargains. A speculator may buy the right to purchase stock at a given price on a given day from another speculator—this is termed purchasing the call; he may obtain the right to sell, compelling the other to buy—this is denominated the "put"—or he may buy the choice between the two, which is called "buying the put or call;" or otherwise, "making a speculation in options." "Backwardation" is a fee paid to have the time of payment deferred; this is sometimes very heavy, and is only resorted to in cases of extreme necessity.

All the business, however, which is done in the Stocks *for time*, is not of a gambling nature. In a place of so extensive commerce as London, opulent merchants, who possess property in the funds, and are unwilling to part with it, have frequently occasion to raise money for a short time. Their resource in this case is to sell for money and buy for account; and although the money raised in this manner costs more than the legal interest, it affords an important accommodation, and may be rendered strictly legal and recoverable.

But, after making all allowance, it must still be confessed that the amount of actual gambling carried on within these precincts is such as to produce mischief of the most terrible extent, equally destructive of fortune, honour, and moral character. If the chronicles of the Stock and Share market could ever be fairly written, they would furnish some of the most frightful histories of crime and its punishment that the world has ever seen. Colossal fortunes overturned, bright prospects blasted, and domestic happiness destroyed—murders, forgery, suicides—would occur in page after page, and the reader would close the volume, at once appalled and disgusted with its revelations.

At a very early period in the history of the Stock Exchange, transactions began to find a place in which an unfair advantage was taken of political position; and this, though at all times counted eminently dishonourable, is believed to occur even still. Such a charge was brought against Sir Robert Clayton, a governor of the Bank of England in the reign of William III., and for many years after one of its directors. It is difficult to decide whether there were any grounds for the accusation.

Another director whose honour was thus impugned was Sir Henry Furnese, one of the most enterprising men of the day. He maintained at his private expense a complete train of intelligence through Holland, Flanders, France, and Germany. In not a few instances he received the news of important events, such as battles, long before the Government; and the fall of Namur, among others, largely added to his profits, owing to his early intelligence. At times he condescended to communicate such intelligence to his Majesty's Ministers, which loyalty King William rewarded on more than one occasion by costly presents. The pamphleteers reproach Sir Henry Furnese with having fabricated news, and having turned his "*Reuter*" agency to the most mercenary account.

It is said that, if Sir Henry wished to buy, his brokers were ordered to look gloomy and mysterious, hint at important news, and even effect sham sales. Their movements were closely watched; the contagion spread; and the speculators having got fairly alarmed, the prices lowered not unfrequently four or five per cent. Now was the time for other agents to buy—of course to the immense benefit of their employer. Similar stories are told of the wealthy Hebrew banker, Medina, who accompanied Marlborough in all his campaigns. It is tolerably well proved that he prevailed upon the avarice of the great commander to accept a regular annuity of six thousand pounds. He largely repaid himself by expresses containing early intelligence of the battles fought; and Ramilies, Oudenarde, Blenheim, administered as much to the purse of the shrewd Hebrew banker as they did to the glory of the English nation.

These proceedings cannot be called gambling—they are something far worse; but the game of chance which is now carried on is more dangerous, because more extensive. This vice, in one form or another, is lamentably on the increase among the lower orders, properly so called—the ill-educated, half-washed, and more than half-criminal classes. Betting on horse-racing is one of its favourite expressions: shopboys and young clerks become corrupted by these scoundrels, and an abundant crop of robberies and small forgeries is the result of the seed thus sown. The class above these have lately added to their turf gambling, that which the outskirts of the Stock Exchange can offer, and have found there precisely what they wanted. It has become notorious that the proceedings carried on with those closed doors on a grand scale have been imitated on a smaller one without, and a sort of unlicensed jobbing has tempted its victims to their ruin.

It was remarked that less interest than usual was felt on the turf on the Derby of 1866; less holiday-making took place at Epsom, because there was a gambling place open, more like a Regent-street "hell," where greater stakes were to be played for, more ruinous "operations" were to be carried on, minus the pure air and the breezy downs. Capel Court was more than a match for the Surrey fields. How many volumes have been written against gambling! What praise has been bestowed on police magistrates when they have dispersed a greasy assembly of vagabonds, and imprisoned perhaps one or two for blocking up Bride Lane, or some other such thoroughfare, in order to carry on their betting transactions. We, too, praise the magistrates, but we should like to ask what would become of the Stock Exchange if its frequenters met with even-handed justice.

"Gambling, my son," says worthy Paterfamilias, "is the ruin of thousands; never let me hear of your making a book; stick to your legitimate business and you will do good and not harm to yourself and others." Very true; but you,

Paterfamilias, have yourself placed your son with Messrs. Bruin and Bear, who, in addition to being stock-brokers, do a pretty considerable amount of time-bargains, and have always a choice collection of rumours ready in store, in whatever direction they choose to speculate. Our mercantile honour has long been the subject of " operations for the fall." Deeds which our fathers would have blushed to name, are now acknowledged without the least confusion; embezzlement, malversation, dishonourable conduct of every kind, are growing terribly common. We no longer regard the best names as security for commercial integrity; the obligations of business are made light of, and what are we to look for next?

It is to be hoped that some steps will be taken to purge our markets from crime, the effects of which are becoming alarming. At present there is a great difficulty in dealing with that class of offenders who, for selfish purposes, propagate mercantile scandal; but something *ought* to be done, and that speedily. Meantime, the best advice to persons concerned is to resist resuscitation of panics. They will probably be attempted. Too much booty has been made by the banditti in that of 1866 not to encourage them to try again; and the rather less guilty pickpockets will be glad to gather another golden harvest such as they had. But better times will come; few firms are really bankrupt; few banks in more than temporary difficulty. A wise and general confidence will speedily restore the tone of the markets, and save many hundreds of thousands of pounds from the hands of robbers; and terrible as the late revelations of fraud have been, it is yet asserted, by those best informed, that commercial crime is not on the increase.

CHAPTER IX.

PRINCIPLES OF COMMERCE—FREE TRADE AND RESTRICTION.

Freedom of Commerce—Instances of—Necessity of Taxation—Employment of Duties: Retaliative Duties, Protective Duties—Chili stockings—Corn Laws, how to be understood Competition—Rent—Colonial Produce—Commerce to be entirely free.

THE principles of commerce will not be discussed here further than as they affect and are affected by those of monetary science. Money is the instrument of universal barter,—the world's common measure of value; whatever, therefore, encourages trade, stimulates the money market; whatever makes money abundant and easy to obtain on reasonable terms, encourages and enlarges commercial operations. If the merchant can trade freely and profitably, it is worth his while to trade; the necessities of his position bring him into the money market, and the banker, the bill discounter, the stock-broker and jobber, participate in his prosperity as well as the shipbuilder and the manufacturer. If on the other hand, restrictions are laid upon him beyond those dictated by absolute necessity, his efforts are relaxed, and all those dependent upon his operations are proportionably restricted in theirs.

Commerce, to fulfil its great objects, must be free, and in proportion as this freedom is really enjoyed among nations, they will be increasingly able to develop their various resources, the more inclined to peace, and the money market will be excited to a more wholesome activity in providing that which was once called the sinews of war, and may be called still more emphatically, the sinews of prosperity. By freedom of commerce, is meant that all who wish to buy, shall buy where they find the best and cheapest articles, and that all who wish to sell, shall have the liberty of selling where they find the most advantageous market. I want oil, wine, and furs; a merchant in the Papal States will supply me with the first, one at Bordeaux with the second, and one at St. Petersburgh with the third. I may have them all of home growth, but the one will be thick and coarse, the other poor and unwholesome, and the last-named neither fine nor durable; those which are offered to me from abroad, are all excellent in their kind. On the other hand, the Italian merchant wants cotton, the French farmer wants machinery, and the Russian fur-dealer wants cutlery. All these things I can supply much better and cheaper than each of my foreign correspondents can make for himself: why should we not exchange? I send abroad, therefore, my home-grown or home-made productions, and receive in return, the produce of foreign lands.

Now that this should be done with regard to all commodities, is the theory of free trade. Founded on nature, it is obviously for the *general* advancement of mankind, but when the theory comes to be applied to practice, we are met with many difficulties, and much opposition. First, the Government says: "We must have money for the service of the public; direct taxation, though best in principle, will not serve us, for no Government would be able to raise by direct taxation the amount required for that purpose in England; we must, therefore, have Customs' duties, and Excise duties." This demand is one which is both just and expedient; let us see how it acts. Suppose that I can buy in Italy a quart of olive oil for sixpence, and suppose that the freight, land-carriage, and profit to merchant and retainer amount to as much more, then if trade were quite free, I should pay one shilling for the same article in London; but there is a duty levied of threepence, which goes to the Government here, and I pay one shilling and threepence to the Italian warehouse-keeper for my bottle of oil. But it may be also that the Papal Government imposes an export duty, that is, does not allow oil to leave the country without first paying somewhat for the permission; let us call this export duty another threepence; I then pay one shilling and sixpence for my bottle of oil, and the payment may be divided somewhat in this manner: sixpence goes to the Italian cultivator, and is the return for his labour and capital; sixpence goes to the shipowners, carriers, merchants, and retailers; threepence, minus the expense of collecting, goes to the British Government, and may be expended in gunpowder and scarlet cloth, or it may help to make up the salary of the Lord-Chancellor, or the pay of policeman B 22. While the remaining threepence may, in like manner, when the expense of collecting is deducted, go towards keeping in prison some unfortunate nobleman who has been detected in reading the Bible. With the uses to which the Papal Government may put their funds, we have, however, no concern here. No government can be carried on without money, nor can any nation be left without government. So long as the duty is a moderate one, it will have little or no effect upon consumption; the foreign grower will find his market, the consumer here the required commodity, and the civil authorities the sums necessary for the public service.

But now let us suppose that the grower of oil at Valencia and Malaga can supply the same article at the same price, and that the Spanish Government imposes no export duty, then the Spanish oil can be sold for fifteenpence. When the Italian oil costs eighteenpence, one fifth, that is, 20 per cent., is added by the Papal Government to the price of this oil, and the article is excluded from the market by legislative restriction. Let us further suppose, that in consequence of a commercial treaty with the States of the Church, a duty is laid on Spanish oil, greater than that paid by the produce of Italy, or that the duty is remitted on the latter and not on the former, the value of the two articles would then be equalized, and they would divide the market; but Spain would immediately impose some retaliative duty on British produce, which would counterbalance, and probably more than counterbalance, the advantages gained by the treaty.

From this it will appear that the imposition of a duty does not necessarily interfere with the freedom of commerce, but only in those cases where the amount imposed excludes desirable commodities. At the same time it is almost a maxim of political economy, that a low rate of duty (on articles of common use) is more productive than a high one; thus there appears reason to believe that, were the present duties on tea and French wines even still more reduced, a larger sum would be paid to the Government, and the comfort and welfare of the people materially augmented. Articles of mere luxury are fair objects of heavy import duties. It matters nothing to the nation at large, and very little either to the foreign producer or the home consumer, that the rich man should pay two or three hundred per cent. duty on his bottle of *Curaçoa* or *Maraschino*—the State is a gainer, and no one is a loser.

From the consideration of import duties simply as means of raising a revenue, we come to regard them in the light of protective enactments. A single stocking-frame was set up some twenty years ago in Santiago, the capital of Chili; the Chilian authorities forthwith, to protect their home-manufacturers, imposed upon all foreign stockings an almost prohibitive duty. This was done with a view to *protect* home-interests. What was the result? The Nottingham stocking-weaver wanted Chilian produce, but he was unable to pay for it, because his payment—that is, his manufactured goods—would not be taken. The Chilian farmer lost his market, and the inhabitants of Santiago were obliged to go without stockings; at least this would have been the effect had so absurd a regulation been persisted in.

But to take a familiar instance: let it be supposed that, under his present circumstances of rental, the English farmer cannot grow corn to remunerate him at less than forty-five shillings a quarter; let it be also supposed that from Poland and Russia corn of equal quality can be sent into the market at forty shillings; the foreigner, in this case, undersells the home-grower by five shillings per quarter. Government lays on a protecting duty of five shillings, and thus equalizes the two articles for the benefit of the English producer. Let us, then, investigate this transaction:—First, we see that the State takes five shillings from the foreigner, in order that the farmers may take five shillings from the British consumer; the weight therefore falls on the public, who are thus taxed because the conditions of farmers are unprosperous. The artisan says to the Government, You make me pay tenpence for the loaf which, were it not for your enactment, I should get for eightpence; and, as other commodities follow, to a great extent, the price of bread, your corn law makes my coat, my tools, and my cottage all dearer to me, while my wages are not in any way raised by it." Now, as the object of this protection duty is to secure the interest of the farmer, *under his present circumstances*, it would be clearly the same thing, so far as he is concerned, to tax the public by a corn law, or to give him direct bounty out of the proceeds of the other taxes to the extent of five shillings in the quarter; in each case, *all* the public would pay it; in each case, the object would be the same; in each case, it would be equally effectual; but in the latter, stripped of its indirect character, it would be an odious and iniquitous piece of favouritism.

But hitherto we have seen the matter only in one light; two questions remain :—Is it so impossible to compete with the foreigner, even under present circumstances? and, secondly, if so, why? The rate at which land continues to be sold, and the continuing eagerness to possess it, would seem to indicate that the impossibility itself is not by any means a self-evident proposition. No one contends that the soil of England and Ireland is less fertile than that of Poland or Russia; the increasing knowledge of agricultural chemistry—a science as yet in its infancy—will probably make our harvests more than sufficient for our wants. In fine, the problem of competition has yet to be solved.

But supposing that it be solved, and solved unfavourably, then comes the other question—Why cannot the English farmer compete with him of Poland or Lithuania? The reply is, he does not live in the same manner, subsist on the same fare; he is more taxed, and, above all, *he pays a higher rent*. Now, no one would wish to degrade the English farmer, to the condition of the Polish serf or the Russian slave; the equalization cannot be made in that manner; and besides, it is to be hoped, on the contrary, that the *less* civilized will gradually be brought up to the level of the *more* civilized; and the equalization of condition will thus be effected. Again, it is not true, to any extent worthy of notice, that the English farmer is more heavily taxed than the foreigner. If direct and indirect taxation be taken together into consideration, it will appear that this country is not more burdened than the generality of continental nations. The third objection is a true and valid one—*he pays a higher rent*. This is a matter which will soon rectify itself; and with its rectification will disappear all the inconveniences which have been supposed indissolubly connected with free trade in corn. It has been strangely forgotten, by many writers, that land is a commodity as well as corn, and that its price, whether for sale or hire, must depend on what can be gained by means of it. If brooms fetch threepence each in the market, the man must be mad who buys the materials for threepence-halfpenny, and then says to the State—I cannot sell my produce save at a loss, to speak nothing of my own support; make up to me the deficiency out of the taxes.

Another case supposed to require protection duties, is that of colonial produce. Other nations and their colonies may undersell us; we must, it is said, protect our colonists, by imposing a duty on produce similar to theirs when it reaches us from other sources. But it is by no means clear that we have a right to lay an extraordinary tax on our home population for the benefit of our colonies. Colonies are established to be an aid, not a burden, to the parent state; and if rightly managed, would be so. Besides which, it is difficult to assign any irremediable cause by which our colonists are undersold, and the wiser plan is not to bolster up a corrupt system by protection duties, but to remove those causes which make free trade unprofitable. It is said that slave labour is so much cheaper than free labour, that our West Indian colonies cannot sell their produce at the same rate as Cuba and Brazil. If this indeed be so, it may be a question between a protection duty which treats negro slavery as an element in prices, and an absolute prohibition of all importation of slave-labour produce, on the ground that the system itself is bad, unchristian, and unlawful.

This principle will find its natural limitations. Where an article is *necessary*, and is only to be obtained in sufficient quantities from states employing slave-labour, then the old maxim, " Necessitas non habet leges," is applicable. But even then a Christian nation will make no small exertion to procure a sufficient supply from the produce of free labour, and will use the other only so long as the absolute necessity remains.

It must never be forgotten that *all* duties fall on the consumer: so long as they do not materially reduce the amount of the article imported, they are a tax on the home population—more or less justifiable in proportion as they affect the necessaries of life. If they do reduce to any considerable extent the amount of importations, then they do to a certain extent affect the comfort of the people, the prosperity of the merchants, and the welfare of foreign producers.

Commerce, to be really free, must be free in *all* its branches; that enactment is but a deliberate injustice which sets only one class of producers free, and holds back the rest by a system of restrictions. If the English farmer be made to stand on a commercial equality with the Pole and the Russian, he ought to be compensated by free access to *all* the products of the known world: whatever he can gain by free trade, is the return made to him for his otherwise reduced profits. The only lawful reason for any import duty is that the support of the State renders it necessary; and then it should be so arranged, so levied, and so collected, as to interfere in the slightest possible degree with the freedom of trade.

As a general principle protection has been long given up in this country and freedom of commerce substituted in its place.

If the subject of this chapter should seem but slightly connected with financial science, let it be remembered that not only do duties and commerce and the money market all reciprocally affect each other, but that the price of our own stocks depend on our commercial prosperity, and the payment of the interest and principal of foreign loans on the customs of great foreign ports.

CHAPTER X.

OF JOINT-STOCK COMPANIES AND LIMITED LIABILITY.

Necessity of New Legislation—Meaning of the term Commandite—Equity of the New Law—Real Liability—Large and Small Shares—Lord Overstone's Opinion—Progress of the Principle—Early Opposition—Joint-stock Banks—their Liability.

For many years a notion was afloat in the financial world that undertakings of decided importance were retarded, and the general course of commerce impeded, by the peculiar liabilities of all who entered into partnership.

If a man shared the profits of a business, however small his share might be, he became to all intents and purposes a partner, and was answerable, to use the powerful phrase current at the time, "to his last acre and his last shilling," for the debts incurred by the firm or company. This, it was contended, prevented hundreds from investing moderate sums in enterprises of great public utility, keeping capital and intellect alike out of the market, and unnecessarily and prejudicially restricting the field of investment.

It was proposed that a plan which had been found to act well in France should be introduced into this country, and that partnership "*en commandite*" should become an English institution. The meaning of this was that any person having a sum, large or small, which he wished to employ in business, might do so without endangering more. This plan was, of course, only applicable to joint-stock companies—the minimum number of partners was to be fixed, but any extension allowed, and it was provided by the Act that no member of such company should be held legally responsible for more than that which he covenanted to pay.

It is difficult to object to an arrangement morally and philosophically so reasonable, and there is no doubt that the system has largely increased the commerce and therefore the prosperity of the country. It has employed, and thereby rendered profitable, immense sums which would otherwise have been hoarded, or what is nearly the same thing, been invested in consols. Losses were less felt when they entailed no further consequences than such as could be clearly foreseen, and ventures were bolder when the extent of the risk was clearly defined. The principles of equity make this indispensable in large companies having numerous shareholders, for as these are necessitated to trust the management of their common business to directors, secretaries, and others, and cannot look after it themselves, they are entitled to say, "We will trust you so much and no more;" and it would be hard upon them to call for larger sums when these have been expended. With regard to the general public engaged in trade, this seems a case in which the maxim "*caveat emptor*" may be fairly applied. In fact, few men of ordinary sagacity trust joint-stock companies of limited liability without having first satisfied themselves of the solvency of the company. But while freely admitting the benefits derived to commerce from this mode of transacting it, I cannot refrain from noticing how much larger are the responsibilities in joint-stock companies than they are sometimes aware of.

A prospectus is sent to me of a new Company. It has a fine name—Albert, or Victoria, or Royal, or Imperial, or something equally high-sounding and as remote from trade. Tables are added which show that the lowest percentage of profit to be realized is far beyond the usual gains of business— ten or twenty, or thirty; that there is absolutely no risk; that the capital is to be two millions; that application must be made at once, or, so great is the pressure for shares, it will be too late. This captivating document further informs me that the shares are £10 each, and it is not considered probable that more than two pounds will be required; one pound to be paid on allotment, and the other shortly afterwards, to carry on the operations of the company. I know little of business, but the thing seems feasible enough. I have heard some of the directors spoken of as mighty men in the City, perhaps even millionaires. I have fifty pounds which I am willing to invest, and I apply for twenty-five shares. The shares are allotted to me, and I pay my twenty-five pounds; soon after I am called upon for another sum of the same amount, and I set my mind at rest, feeling that I am not, " in all probability," to be called on for any further contribution.

But the real state of the case is this:—I have made myself actually liable for £250. If the company prosper, they will want to call up the rest of their capital, to enlarge and improve their business; if unsuccessful, they will have to make calls to cover their responsibilities. Nor can I, by the simple process of selling my shares (that is, if I can sell them), release myself from my liability. One twelvemonth must pass before my transfer frees me from the possibility of further calls, or "contributions," in case the company should "wind up." And here, too, is a further safeguard for those with whom it may contract debts, a class of persons for whom sometimes a greater amount of sympathy is expressed than their positions require.

A very able writer on the subject of limited liability expresses himself as follows:—

"The law of 'limited liability' is exceedingly defective in one of its chief elements, and it requires to be 'limited' itself in one very important particular—viz., the amount of uncalled capital. No company ought to have a certificate of 'limited liability' unless the shares are issued on the principle of being paid up at least one-half—say 50 per cent. of the nominal amount. If this had been adopted, much of the alarm and distress of unfortunate shareholders would have been simply impossible. Most people would prefer shares of small denominations paid up in full; but if that be thought too severe a restriction, certainly one-half should be paid. The intention of Parliament was to sanction and protect the joint employment of private *capital*, not joint *credits;* and the departure from this principle will always be fraught with danger.

"It may be said in reply, the law leaves it open. The law should not leave it open, inasmuch as ninety-nine persons out of every hundred are not aware of the dangers they incur; and the law ought to be wisely framed, so as to protect the ninety-nine per cent. of unthinking or ignorant persons who may have small capitals to invest."

It is evident that what is required is a limitation of excessive liability whilst the company is in its infancy, and increasing it as the company makes progress. The plan of companies limited by guarantee will be found the best suited for effecting this improvement. To exemplify the method of obtaining it, the capital of a guarantee company should be separated into two parts—viz., the paid-up capital, and the guarantee capital.

The guarantee capital is purely a liability, and the company cannot call it up. It is only a guarantee fund for creditors, to come into operation in case the company suspends. The advantage of this cannot be overrated. By assuring to creditors an exclusive fund, to be divided rateably among them, guarantee companies will never find any difficulty in obtaining support and credit to carry on their operations. A company formed in the following manner would, probably, be found to work excellently.

We will say a bank is to be established, which

in the usual way would be formed with a capital of £1,000,000, in 10,000 shares of £100 each.

It should be shaped as follows :—

Number of shares, £10,000.

Total limit of amount of each share, £100.

Half thereof working capital (liable to be called up) £50.

Half thereof guarantee capital, £50.

Of these amounts, shareholders should incur liability for such.

Shareholders are hardly yet awakened to the fact that companies having £50 shares, with £5 or £10 paid, are practically unlimited. A company's shares must always be fixed at an amount commensurate with the extent of business it intends or hopes to do, and no provision is made for shareholders incurring a less amount of liability, whilst the company is advancing towards the summit of its ambition. Although in its earlier stages its transactions must be small, shareholders incur precisely the same amount of liability which they will incur when the company has attained full vigour, is doing an extensive business and paying profits accordingly. Thus, not only do shareholders incur a great risk without return, but the amount of their liability gives the company a fictitious kind of credit, and encourages directors to enter into transactions not in keeping with the paid-up capital and standing of the company, and which, on the slightest disturbance of the commercial world, provokes its downfall. It is sometimes said, " have fully paid-up shares;" but a company must needs have some small credit, it cannot possibly carry on business, having to pay from hand to mouth, and a company with fully paid-up shares in these days has no credit whatever.

Formerly confidence in the integrity of the directors would ensure a little, but that is now at a great discount. If such part only of the working capital as is actually called, and of the corresponding amount of guarantee capital—at first, say, when £5 per share is called up, then the real capital would be £50,000 working capital, £50,000 guarantee capital; with £10 called up, £100,000 working capital and £100,000 guarantee capital, and so on until the amount of capital as registered is called up, when, if further capital is required, a fresh issue of shares should be made—the calling up of capital under these circumstances amounts in effect to a power of increasing the capital by increasing the amount of the shares up to a certain limit named in the articles. The power to increase the number of shares, does not put the shareholders under any liability until they have actually resolved

K

on the increase. Of course the proportion of working and guarantee capital might be greater or less than one-half, according to the nature of the company. Thus the responsibility of shareholders would from time to time be exactly in ratio to the amount of business the company was doing; as that increased calls would become necessary, so that the amount of their liability would increase to a fixed amount, and directors of new companies would not be able to enter into the transactions which have recently proved the downfall of so many companies.

We have now had eleven years' trial of limited liability, the Act authorizing it having received the Royal assent in the autumn of 1855. The time has come when the whole Act might with advantage receive a revision; but the alterations required are merely matters of detail, and it is hardly likely that the principle will ever be called in question.

Regarding the *rationale* of a joint-stock company with limited liability merely as an enlargement of the old one of partnership, and differing from it simply by the introduction of this necessary limitation, there are several questions which at first appear merely of detail, but which, when carefully examined, will be found to involve principles, and some of great magnitude. With a few of these we must briefly deal.

Should a joint-stock company divide its stock into small shares or large ones—this is an important question—small shares attract small shareholders, and large ones the reverse. The capital may be the same in both cases; but the larger body, which is of course that of the small shareholders, will be necessarily more fluctuating than the smaller constituency, and in consequence of this the value of the shares will be more fluctuating also. This is a disadvantage, and one which makes companies of this kind eminently distasteful to great capitalists. On the other hand, the broader basis is on the whole quite as *secure* as the narrower one; and if it be advisable to induce the middle classes to invest their savings in this kind of company, there can be no doubt that the only way to effect this object is to frame the system of shares so that they may be at once within the reach, and suitable to the circumstances, of this class of investors. All that tends to extend a knowledge of mercantile affairs—to employ capital to the greatest *general* advantage—should be encouraged by those who desire to promote the welfare of the nation at large. The pence of the poor may do their part with the fifty-pound notes of the rich; and as there is nothing more prejudicial than the system of hoarding, so there is nothing more advantageous, in a moral as in a financial point of view, than the judicious investment of savings.

Among great capitalists, however, such opinions are not held. They look at investments from their own stand-point; they wish, for the most part, only to be associated with the leviathans of the money market; and they have, with few exceptions, set themselves against the principles of joint-stock associations and limited liability. If it were impossible to enter into companies which effect large commercial transactions without taking large shares, which at once require extensive capital and entail corresponding risks; if, in case of non-success, each shareholder were liable to his last shilling or his last acre,—none but wealthy men could undertake the responsibility.

Under the old system this was the case, and its natural tendency was to make great houses greater, rich men richer, and to abolish gradually what may be termed the middle classes of commerce. In fact, mercantile operations became so gigantic that these last were in a fair way of being crushed out altogether; there was no room for them; and just as they were about to disappear the joint-stock principle came to their aid, and enabled them to make head against what had been hitherto out-buying, out-selling, and out-financing them. Now it is clear that the principles of joint-stock trade, which is only an enlarged kind of partnership, and those of limited liability, must stand or fall together. All contracts must be free if commerce is to flourish. No unnecessary interference on the part of Government is to stand in the way of its development. The tendency of the age is so far a wholesome one as it is towards a removal of all restrictions on trade, of what kind soever they may be, and to leave it to the natural effect of its own operations.

But if a company is clearly at liberty to frame its system of shares on such a scale as it may deem best, may it not alter that scale according to the requirements of its shareholders? May it not say to these, At present your shares are shares of £20 each; we wish to double the number of these, and at the same time to reduce the value of each share by one-half. Thus A. B., who has twenty shares, the collected value of which is £400, will have forty shares of £10 each, amounting in value to the same sum. Nothing can be simpler than this, and nothing can seem fairer than that the company should have power to effect the change. But, as the law now stands, it cannot do this without a new charter. Application was made for an alteration of the law in this respect, and (mainly through the instrumentality of the great capitalists, with Lord Overstone at their head), the bill for the change was thrown out. The grounds of the refusal may be briefly stated thus:—That by this change the whole character of the constituency would be altered, and that those who purchase £20 shares do so with the understanding that they are co-operating with a class of investors having certain elements of stability; that the understanding is broken if the value of the share be altered, and a new constituency be introduced. In fact, that the change is much like the reduction of the parliamentary franchise, and susceptible of being defended or opposed on similar grounds. Under these circumstances the bill was rejected by the House of Lords in the present month (June, 1866).

Joint-stock banks are capable of adopting the principle of limited liability, but only with regard to their business as banks of deposit. Such as have the privilege of issuing notes are of unlimited liability as regards such issue. Thus, if I hold a five-pound note of the West Diddlesex Bank,—a joint-stock bank formed out of the private business of Messrs. Slap, Dash, Hazard, and Crasher,—I can, on the failure of such a bank, obtain my five pounds out of the private property of the partners, though I could not make them pay me my deposits beyond the amount which their shares when paid up would furnish.

Joint-stock banking met with great opposition when the system was new. The private banks refused even to acknowledge the new corporations, and the directors of the Bank of England acted steadily against them for many years. Now the principle seems acknowledged on all hands to have been a great success, and to be eminently suited to the exigencies of the time.

CHAPTER XI.

DISCOUNT AND FINANCE COMPANIES.

Nature of Discount Companies—Nature and Origin of Finance Companies—Their vast Designs—Examples from the Turkish Empire—Danger of distant Enterprises—Perils of Finance Companies—Aid to Railways—Prospects of the Principle.

DISCOUNT companies will require but little explanation here; their business is to discount bills, and this they transact, or should transact, on the same principles as do private bill-brokers. The profession is an extremely lucrative one, but as its great profits depend on the judgment and financial skill of the brokers, it is one which should only be undertaken by such as feel they have these requisite qualifications in a more than usual degree. Hence it is less adapted to be worked by a company than most others, as it must ultimately depend for success on the individual ability of its managers. Bankers are always bill-discounters, and when they have been brought into difficulties, it has often been by errors in this branch of their business. As the discount varies with the character of the bills offered, as well as the condition of the market of the time, the capacity to seize and combine all the circumstances of the paper, requires at once a powerful memory, a keen judgment of character, an accurate knowledge of money affairs, and of business in general, and a power forecasting future events, as connected with mercantile transactions, which few possess in perfection.

The nature of a bill of exchange has been already explained. The holders of these acceptances take them to bankers or bill-brokers, and secure for them cash, minus the rate of discount agreed upon. But it is not to be inferred that the market has no rule for this rate, or that if various rates be charged there is anything necessarily unfair in it. For, on the one hand, the Bank itself fixes the rate at which it will transact discount business, and this varies with the state of the market, sometimes reaching as high as 10 or even 11 per cent., and sometimes falling as low as $2\frac{1}{2}$. On the other hand, there is a vast amount of paper brought into the market, which neither the bank nor any house of eminence can even look at, and this is taken up by speculators of all classes, and forms a hazardous and sometimes discreditable kind of business, which is nevertheless often highly remunerative. Thus the rate of discount is various, for even on the best paper the bank rate is generally a little higher than that of the market in general. It will usually be found that with the rate of discount as charged by the bank, the funds rise and fall, another proof of the close connexion existing between monetary and commercial interests, between cash and trade, between the bank and the country. Discount companies are taking the place of private bill-discounters, just as joint-stock banks are of private bankers, and if due care be taken in the selection of managers, and those managers exert all their faculties and all their diligence, there seems no reason to doubt that they will have an equal success.

Finance companies are a new kind of power. They are to work the same results as the great capitalists have hitherto done—they undertake to supply cash for the most gigantic undertakings, they make railways, tunnel under mountains, build cities, establish great public works, assist vast enterprises, and do with their huge capital what few even among millionaires can accomplish alone. Such an idea is a grand one, and it is by no means improbable that the world owes it to the brain of the most subtle thinker and energetic actor of the age—the Emperor Napoleon III. While, however, no one can doubt the magnitude of the idea, or the extent of its probable results, it must be understood that the risks are proportionate, and companies of this kind are peculiarly liable to the operations of panic-makers. If successful, their profits must necessarily be immense; if otherwise, the losses will be tremendous. In regarding these associations as offering investments, it must be noticed that they do not communicate their plans to their shareholders, except in a very general way, so that no man can properly judge for himself as to the probabilities of success or failure.

As a specimen of what may sometimes be done, I take the following report of an Oriental undertaking, very recently commenced. It has some evident elements of success. No country is richer in natural resources than Turkey; nowhere are legitimate profits greater; no nation has a higher character for integrity. When, therefore, a company was formed to develop the profit-producing powers of such an empire, it is scarcely to be wondered at that it should speedily give tokens of success. Still, there is something astonishing and a little suspicious in such a statement as that actually put forth by the company. It runs thus:—

"The first report of the *Société Générale de l'Empire Ottoman*, which was founded in 1864 by the Imperial Ottoman Bank, and some of the leading Turkish and Greek houses connected with the East, has been received. The company seems completely to have realized so far the anticipations which were originally formed respecting it. The net profits for the eighteen months embraced in the accounts referred to in the report, a period which includes the time occupied in establishing the company, have been £335,000, equal to nearly 31 per cent. per annum on the capital paid up from time to time; and the dividend which is now to be distributed is £2 per share, leaving a balance of over £5000 to be carried forward. This dividend does not include nearly £32,000 placed to reserve, and about 10s. per share already divided amongst the shares. The report and accounts (a translation of which can be had at the Imperial Ottoman Bank) are most interesting to all connected with Turkey. To one remark in the report we can direct attention with satisfaction—viz., that the whole of the profits now to be divided have actually been realized."

This may or may not be true, and the prospects thus held out may or may not be fulfilled; but two things are certain. One is, that the resources of a country so rich and so undeveloped as Turkey are fully equal to produce such results as are here indicated; and another is, that what may be called the *natural* interest of money is greater in countries only partially cultivated than in the old and highly civilized communities of Europe. Ten per cent. in such countries is the usual rate, and being so the actual profit on its employment may be reasonably estimated at something much higher—nor would another twenty per cent. be an unreasonable expectation. At the same time, the distance of such lands from our own—the lax notions of commercial morality which too frequently prevail among their inhabitants, the difficulty of obtaining redress in case of fraud, and many other drawbacks, must be taken into account when we contemplate entering into speculations of this nature.

Finance companies are, as I have already said, the grandest productions of modern commerce, and they are also the most speculative. Hence they require the greatest care and the most extensive information on the part of those who are to conduct them. They have another disadvantage which they share with all joint-stock companies more or less; and that is, that it is comparatively easy to get up "bubble" companies of this description. Few persons know much of the real grounds on which a company is formed; the public puts its faith in the principal names on the direction, and these have often been either fraudulently obtained or boldly printed without their owners' consent. It is a notorious fact that a company was formed by three penniless adventurers, who could not among them pay for a luncheon at a tavern where they met to frame their prospectus; and yet they "floated" their company, and it ultimately became prosperous;—but then the scheme was a good one.

But finance companies are especially subject to danger, if they pass out of their legitimate field of operation. They ought never to be subject to "a run," and ought therefore to eschew all deposits save for considerable periods. Most of those which suffered in the late panic did so by not adhering to this rule. Their *business* is to have their capital "locked up," and to be subject to no demand save for dividends. They require also peculiar care, on the part of shareholders, to have satisfactory and searching examinations into the state of their affairs, and it is the duty of these, in case of any irregularity, to deal stringently with managers, secretaries, directors, and auditors.

The following details of a case tried before Vice-Chancellor A. B. will exhibit the need of such vigilance. A morning paper of a certain date not long since, gives them thus :—

"This was a motion for an injunction to restrain C. D. from purchasing with the company's money any further shares in the company, or in any other company which the directors of the X. Y. are not justified in purchasing by its articles of association. The bill alleged, that although the company was forbidden by its articles of association from purchasing its own shares, C. D. had previously to the last general meeting, on the —— of ——, purchased more than 20,000 of its shares at premiums varying from £—— to £—— per share out of the funds of the company; that if the shares increased in value C. D. resold them, and appropriated the profits; if they declined he allowed the shares to remain in the names of his nominees as trustees for the company. The bill contained further allegations, that C. D. out of the company's funds purchased upwards of 12,000 shares in the Z. Improvements V. Company (1750 being registered in the name of F. G., and 2349 in the name of H. I., two of the clerks of the X. Y., and 350 in the name of J. K., a clerk in the employment of C. D., and a stockbroker); and the plaintiffs further alleged, that in case the company should be wound up, the *bonâ fide* shareholders would not have the benefit of any contribution whatever from the persons in whose names the shares so purchased stand, as such persons were in humble means and wholly unfit to pay calls; that L. M. had spent upwards of £200,000 in buying shares in the Imperial Land Company of W., and that they had bought large numbers of shares in the U. Freehold Land and Docks Company, in the S. T. Railway, and in the Q. R. Coal Company, all these purchases being entirely unwarranted by the articles of association, and for the purpose of 'rigging the market,' that the shares so purchased had been included among the assets of the company in its balance-sheet, while they were in fact entirely valueless, and involved it in heavy liabilities. Other charges against the defendants were, that they had occasioned ruinous losses to the company; that they had appropriated profits made with the company's moneys to their own use. C. D. was further charged with receiving from the Z. Improvements Company a large sum in cash, for having used his influence with the company to induce his co-directors to introduce the defendants' company, and that C. D. and L. M. had shared such money between them."

It is true that these charges were indignantly denied, and it is no province of the mere chronicler to doubt the truth of the denial, but similar charges were made against many companies, and they aided greatly to keep up and intensify the recent panic.

The very nature of a finance company requires a greater amount of reticence than is necessary in most others. Were their plans all divulged the directors would never be allowed to carry out any one; their whole time would be spent in discussions, all fruitless, and all expensive. Few shareholders would be competent to advise, and all would take upon them to interfere. This reticence is, however, by no means an element of danger. It happens that those very companies in which there is the least probability of trouble or interference on the part of shareholders, are precisely those which to a discriminating mind have the best chances of success. We must except, however, those cases in which a company is formed out of an old private business, supposed to be fortunate. These speculations are quite as often failures as successes. In the first place, there is the antecedent improbability that a flourishing concern will be given up by those who possess it. In the next, there is the inconsistency of such persons remaining to manage a firm for others, which they have, as it is presumed, conducted with a profit all their own. There is little danger of interference on the part of shareholders here, for it is an ominous and significative circumstance, that in the share-list will rarely be found the names of persons engaged in any similar occupation.

But to return to finance companies. They are subject, of course, to most, if not all, of the dangers to which other commercial associations are liable, and they have some which are peculiar to themselves. They suffer from foreign intrigues and diplomacy, from the vicissitudes of war, from the non-fulfilment of foreign obligations, and these because many of those undertakings for which they furnish the means, are in foreign lands, and subject to foreign conditions. At the same time, they are frequently, by the imprudence of their managers, victimized considerably at home. Here is an instance, imaginary indeed, but one which is by no means merely so. It is taken from an able and well-known periodical:—

A railway contractor finds that he is in want of funds with which to conclude the contracts. On application to the company to which the line belongs, he meets with a frank avowal that what between fare expenses, surveying fees, engineers' charges, and other outlays, their balance with their bankers is in a state of collapse. What is to be done? To go on without money is impossible; to declare his inability to proceed is bankruptcy and ruin. In place of hard cash, will the directors give him a certain amount in debentures paid up, or paid-up shares, upon the future line? Of course they will—are delighted to do so—in other words, they virtually discount the future problematical profits of a line not yet made, or, at any rate, not finished. It is as if a young man, newly appointed to a commission in the army, should pay for his outfit by bills which would fall due when he shall become a captain in the service. But anything is better than to stop the works of the railway. To place debentures bearing four, five, or even six per cent., and which are only payable after a term of years, with the general public, is an impossibility. What sane man would dream of investing in such securities with consols at 88, and finance companies paying 40 per cent.? But these securities serve the purpose of the contractor, who has undertaken far more than his capital justified him in doing, and his employers are equally pleased to pay him on these terms.

But of what use are these debentures to a man whose chief outlay is the weekly wages he has to pay? Navvies, even if they could be made to understand the nature of such securities, could hardly be induced to take them in lieu of their weekly wages. But the contractor has no intention of making any attempt to palm off the paper he holds upon the rough giants he employs. With, say, £50,000 of these debentures in his hand, he betakes himself to the "Universal Finance and Comprehensive Credit Company, Limited;" and after one or two interviews with the general manager, his pecuniary arrangements are completed. By depositing these debentures for £50,000 with the "Universal Finance," he obtains the acceptances of that company to sundry small bills, drawn in sums of perhaps £500, and amounting to a total perhaps of £30,000, thus leaving a margin on the security of £20,000.

But though nothing could be more satisfactory than this on paper, yet it is evident that these bills must be continually renewed till either the railway itself is complete, and begins to pay, or till some catastrophe occurs to the financial company. If the latter has been well managed, and has had few transactions of the kind, then this, as an exceptional proceeding, may pass; but if it be a specimen of the company's operations, they will before long clash, and railway and finance company will go down together. The error will have been in taking obligations which required speedy fulfilment, and balancing these with securities which could only be realized at long periods. But, after all, if any great works are to be carried out in the coming age, it will be the new Finance Company principle which will have to accomplish them. It is the widest and grandest development of the limited liability system which has been witnessed; and it is as likely to be as useful to the age which wonders at it, as it is magnificent in itself.

CHAPTER XII.

PANICS AND THEIR CONSEQUENCES.

Nature of a Panic—Various Causes—Operations for the Fall—Bank Failures—How Caused—Hints to Shareholders—Effect of Wise Conduct on the part of the Public—Maxims of the late Duke of Wellington—Description of a Panic.

WHAT is a panic? It is a wild, groundless, unreasoning, and unreasonable terror. It once paralysed statesmen, and defeated armies, and destroyed dynasties. Now it for the most part contents itself with causing banks to close, merchants to fail, and finance companies to make calls on their shareholders; it brings ruin to speculators, embarrassment to contractors, and poverty to families. There is, therefore, quite as much mischief effected now as there was when persons of high degree were the ostensible victims. We have just passed through such a season in London; and, as we would gladly help those who look a little before them, we venture to express an opinion that we have not yet seen the last of it, and we think that those concerned will do well to be prepared for a relapse. Yet there is no reason in the nature of things why this should be. There is very little that is unsound in the present condition of business; perhaps taken on the whole it was never more satisfactory; but the crisis which is now passing away favourably has had a cause which is no secret; and, knowing this, we do not consider a little caution altogether to be despised.

It is generally understood that the late panic was to no small extent the deliberate work of speculators for the fall, or, as they have been more accurately denominated, *operators* for the fall. To a great many of our readers this will be intelligible enough, but the nature and work of the money market is so little understood by the multitude, that we shall take on ourselves to offer a few illustrations of a subject very interesting to the initiated, and equally dry to all beside. An "operator for the fall" is one who wishes, for his own personal benefit, to bring down the value of securities, so as to throw them on the market in large amounts, and at a low price. This may be done by those who wish to buy largely for investment, or by those who intend to make fictitious sales. To accomplish his object the "*operator*" circulates rumours prejudicial to the Government whose stock he desires to depreciate, or the firm or company whose shares he traffics in. " Jacob Omnium is about to resign the chairmanship. I have it from a sure source. He knows which way the wind blows, and he is quietly throwing all his West Diddlesex on the market." "They do say that Baron Redshield has refused aid to the Cursitor-street Finance and Discount, and it is quite certain they can get no assistance from Grubber and Grabber." "Have you heard the last telegram from Paris! The Emperor has agreed to recall his troops from Mexico, and a filibustering expedition is by this time on its way to the frontier. Seward has given the leaders his assurance that they shall not be interfered with, and Maximilian has ordered the Palace at Miramar to be got ready for his reception." So far as these rumours are credited, down go West Diddlesex, Cursitor-street, and Mexicans. People who only judge by the articles in the papers take fright accordingly, sacrifice their shares in bank, company, or foreign stock, and the speculators make their own market. Few persons, save those on the spot, can imagine how sensitive a thing the money market is, and how far a well-imagined calumny will travel, or what amount of mischief it will do before its falsehood is discovered. Never was this diabolical act carried to so great a pitch of perfection as at the present time; never did a few ingenious lies work such widespread devastation. Dr. Watts, in one of his innocent hymns, says—

> Bolts and bars can secure me from robbing and wrong,
> But nought can protect from a liar's vile tongue.

Like a celebrated classical prayer, half the doctor's assertion has been dismissed to the four winds of heaven; bolts and bars wont protect one against Mr. Caseley; but the other half of the poet's distich remains in all its truth. It is said by well-informed persons that from twenty to thirty brokers deliberately set themselves to run down Overend, Gurney, and Co., and effected it! This company is far from being the only one which has met with similar treatment, and to combinations of this sort, men of experience have no hesitation in attributing the severity of the recent crisis. There is no doubt that many unsound speculations were afloat, many houses in business insolvent; but these were not the only sufferers. Firms that could have gone on, tided over their difficulties, furnished safe investments, and carried on a long, enduring, and valuable business, were utterly destroyed.

From the example both of the Agra and Masterman's Bank, and of the Consolidated, it will be clear to those who shall chronicle the panic of 1866, that no amount of reputation on the part of directors and managers was sufficient to protect the firm marked for destruction. It was emphatically said of the latter bank that its directors were "solid, responsible men—rich, and up to their eyes in large affairs; some of them, who, like Mr. Smith, had managed millions, or like Mr. Pender, had built up first-class fortunes by their own skill and daring; or like the Messrs. Hankey, had been bankers from their youth up." Yet this very board did what any bankruptcy lawyer would have told them was a very doubtful one in respect of legality. They agreed to take over the business of another bank which had given way—that is, to take part of the assets, and pay part of the creditors. They would pay deposits, but not acceptances. Of course, this intention was disputed; holders of acceptances insisted on being paid; and the miseries of unsuccessful litigation were added to those of rash speculation. But though there was so able a Board of Directors, and so large a subscribed capital, the whole history of the case showed that the managers made as many blunders as it was well possible for them to make, and that to gratify the demand for immense dividends, they undertook equally immense risks. But they were in a great degree the victims of their own shareholders. We need not contend with some that 4 per cent. is better than 40, but we may be quite sure that when the prospect is held out of obtaining an abnormally large percentage, the shareholders of a joint-stock company should look carefully into their securities, and rather hold back their directors than urge them into untrod, and probably dangerous, paths. When under such circumstances as these, a panic is created—no matter by whom, or with what object—a bank or company has no chance of recovery.

Nor in enumerating the many evils which arise out of panics, must we omit to mention the great inconvenience which the public suffer from large sums of money being locked up in monetary companies under liquidation. At such time men in business are distressed, not so much from having lost some of their money, as from having been suddenly deprived, although, perhaps, only for a time, of the use of all their available cash. On Saturday nights masters cannot pay their workmen, and even private individuals are placed in an awkward position from their inability to command a single shilling. This difficulty can be easily met by the liquidator granting to the creditor on his releasing his debt a certificate of indebtedness payable to bearer, or where the sum is large, a number of certificates representing the total amount. These certificates would be immediately marketable at a price, and also available as security. Debtors to the estate, and shareholders having calls to pay, would be glad to purchase these certificates to extinguish their liabilities, and thus the company would gradually liquidate itself. The plan has been adopted in the case of Overend, Gurney and Co., and was perfectly successful.

Panics often arise from commercial ignorance, and especially from two prevailing errors—one of which is, that wealth and money are synonymous terms; the other is, that in commercial transactions there are two opposing interests involved—that of the buyer, and that of the seller.

The national wealth of a country abounding, like our own, in coal, iron, tin, lead, and copper—in cereals and cattle—in fish, wool, and flax—must entitle it to the appellation of a rich country, even though there were not a coin in it. France, with her boundless store of corn, wine, and oil, is of her own nature wealthy; and money is in such countries only the medium of exchange by which wealth is made available. It is quite possible for a man to have a fertile estate, often of many thousand acres, and yet to have only a balance of one hundred pounds at his banker's; but he does not on such grounds cease to be a rich man. Now what is true of nations and private men, is true also of merchants and mercantile associations. In fact, the truth is self-evident; and it would be almost ridiculous to insist upon it, were it not that so much of our commercial distresses arises from its being ignored or forgotten. A credit, or finance company, possesses securities to the amount of a million sterling. These form its *wealth;* but these cannot, in their very nature, be prematurely turned into cash. Its members have invested their money in them, in order that it may fructify; and to draw out that money till it has done what they invested it to do, is the trick of a child who pulls up the flower he has planted, to see how it is " getting on." All mercantile business must be carried on in a spirit of confidence. Money *and time* are its elements, and the result is *wealth.*

An opinion has lately obtained, that all our recent embarrassments have arisen from "*over-trading,*" and some newspapers have been lecturing the public on this topic, and preaching a kind of crusade against Finance and Credit Companies, as particularly guilty of this great commercial sin; but have not been good enough to tell us what "*over-trading*" means. We should define it thus:— It is the entering into arrangements which the contractor has no *legitimate* means of meeting. A company purchases, with money entrusted to its discretion, a tract of land—say in Brazil, for instance —rich in mineral wealth and in timber, fitted for the production of cotton and cocoa, and advantageously placed with regard to the sea. It wants capital to develop its resources. This the Company supplies. The scheme begins to prosper— shares rise in the market—dividends increase. Now occurs a panic. Reports are diligently spread that the prosperity is all fictitious; the shareholders have been deceived; the great men who joined the company are leaving it; weak holders—that is, those who hold a few shares, and are afraid of a call—take alarm. Country holders hear of the decline, and make inquiries. Too often they also, with the idea of realizing something out of their venture, even if they sacrifice the rest, sell out at a loss. Speculators effect fictitious shares at low prices, and thus frighten those who read the money articles in the daily papers, and the fall goes on. There is a run upon the deposits, property cannot be converted into cash fast enough to satisfy the demand, and the result is—a "crash." Now, it is impossible for one bank, or company, or great house, to fall alone. These business transactions are so blended, too, that the ruin of one must entail that of others likewise; the panic increases, and widespread destruction is the result. Certain of our own papers are *said*, it is to be hoped incorrectly, to have been among the chief "*operators for the fall;*" and the curious but incorrect reports which they occasionally circulate, make it necessary for men of business to be very cautious, and to make very close inquiries before they act upon them. For, *canards* as they are, they do still considerably affect the price of securities on our Exchange. It is true that their influence is diminishing, and will soon be rendered all but innocuous; but what has been done by one agency may be done by another; and it is above all things necessary to remember, that it is by such means that the most deplorable kind of gambling is perpetuated.

The following observations from an eminent financial writer are quite to the present purpose: he says, "those who act in concert to depress the shares of financial companies and banks, to suit their own purposes, bring themselves within the reach of an indictment for conspiracy." It is a matter of notoriety that regular combinations have for some time past been formed for the purpose of making money by sending down shares in the market. The *modus operandi* is as follows: they select the company which is to be the victim of their nefarious plotting, and then unite in seeking by every possible means to withdraw public confidence from it. At first they were tolerably cautious in their operations, confining themselves chiefly to fictitious sales among themselves, which were subsequently quoted as genuine in the price lists; but recently, growing bolder by impunity, they have resorted to more daring and speedier methods of shaking public confidence in the stability of the company against which they are operating. Printed notices are scattered broadcast in the City, advising depositors to withdraw their balances. Circulars are sent to shareholders, counselling them to sell out without delay. The effect of all this, combined with the critical state of affairs, is to cause a run upon the doomed establishment, which, sooner or later, results in a stoppage. The conspirators pocket their paltry gains,—gains procured by entailing ruin and misery upon hundreds—and *da cano!*

There can be little doubt that these and kindred operations constitute a complete conspiracy. What is the definition of a conspiracy? "A combination or agreement between several persons to carry into effect a purpose hurtful to some individual or to the public at large." What can be more hurtful to the shareholders of a company than to depreciate the value of its shares? What can be more hurtful to the public at large than to depreciate without reason shares which are a vendible commodity in the public market? An agreement or combination is entered into to depress shares: what is it but a conspiracy? What are those who are concerned in it but conspirators, and indictable accordingly? If several persons determine to sell out of a company, because they have doubts of its stability and no longer think it a desirable investment, the carrying out of their determination might probably result in depressing the shares of the company, but as they acted *bonâ fide* they would commit no offence. If they agreed however, to sell out of the company, simply to depress the shares for purposes of their own, they would act *mala fide*, and would, I think, be indictable for conspiracy.

Granting that these combinations are illegal, and that those who take part in them can be indicted for conspiracy, it is said that it is difficult to obtain sufficient proof. It is certainly not an easy thing to obtain evidence of conspiracy, but the greater the number of persons engaged in it the greater the facility there is for finding it out. But it is not *impossible* to detect a conspiracy even where great care has been taken to conceal its operations, for some of the conspirators will generally be found ready to save themselves by turning Queen's evidence. In the case of the conspirators in the City, no great difficulty would be found, in collecting evidence in proof of their operations, their clerks, messengers, and porters must have some inkling of their proceedings, and a reward of £1000 would be a tempting bait. The printers of the memorandum and notices flying about in the City would come forward if properly remunerated. Strong suspicion would attach to large buyers after a sudden and unexpected fall, and the city detectives have tripped up cleverer fellows ere now than the bears. But these are only hints. Cannot an association or body of persons be found, who, from motives of interest or public spirit, will take the matter in hand? If successful, they will earn the gratitude of thousands, they will save many a tottering company, will reinstate financial affairs upon their legitimate and sound basis. Even if they fail, which I think is extremely unlikely, they will not have wasted their time or their money, for the circumstance that the law is on the alert will have a very salutary effect in deterring the culprits. Why is the Bankers' Association quiescent? Why do not the respectable members of the Stock Exchange start a fund and engage competent legal assistance thoroughly to sift the affair?

The laws of finance teach us that, wealth and money not being convertible terms, a banker may trade with three-fourths of the capital in his hands. Over-trading, then, means going beyond this; but if a panic be created, then a house which has never over-traded may be forced to close—not by any fault of its own, but by that of the creators of the panic.

We come, then, to the question, How can a panic be prevented, or stopped when already existing? The latter is almost impossible; though something, as we will presently show, may be done even then. But prevention is not only better—it is also easier—than cure; and the physician who knows the cause of disease is far more likely to cure it than one who goes blindly to work. Admitting, what can hardly be doubted in modern times, that a panic is created for the purposes of gain, by parties whose greed of gold is utterly careless of the ruin they cause, and that operations for the fall or rise, as the case may be, are among the chief instruments by which they work, it will be plain that the Legislature and the Stock Exchange, acting together, might render much of the fraud now perpetrated impossible; and that a still further diminution of its success might be effected if the public would second both in carrying out such regulations as might be made to that effect.

And first, the impunity with which at present a broker contracts to sell shares which he does not possess should be entirely removed. He should be compelled to specify the shares he disposes of, and to give the dates of the whole transaction; and the omission of this might be made penal.

The Stock Exchange might refuse to ratify all transfers in which sufficient formalities were not gone through. It is much to be regretted that the Stock Exchange Committee have declined to insist on this, and though a bill is to be brought into the House of Commons to effect the object, yet it will be, in all probability, defeated by the agency of the Stock Exchange.

Purchasers however may insist on having such particulars, and on having their shares or stock on the day specified, and not be put off on any pretence whatever. These measures would be a check on operators, and a security for genuine investors; but the chief reliance of the public must be on themselves.

The following extract from the *Standard* newspaper, referring to the money market, on June 13th, shows the soundness of the preceding observations, and gives hope of a better state of things:—

"The great feature of the day was the rise in the shares of the London and County Bank, owing to the 'Bears,' who sold so largely a day or two previously, being unable to supply the purchasers with the security at the settlement which commenced on that morning. The dilemma in which the small clique, whose operations have lately been the principal cause of the ruin of thousands of shareholders, was placed, has occasioned general satisfaction. Many of these gentlemen who succeeded, a week before, in reducing the value of the shares to £62, were compelled to give £72 for them, or to a backwardation of £5, and in some cases as much as £7 and £9 for the loan of the security for a fortnight. These rates were quite unprecedented; and it is hoped that their effect will be to teach a moral lesson to those who have so ruthlessly endeavoured to damage the property and prospects of their neighbours.

There are a few maxims which seem to be forgotten when chiefly they ought to be remembered. "Nothing venture, nothing have," is one; and another is that famous one of the late Duke of Wellington, "High interest means bad security." Now, all commercial companies—banking, finance, discount, mercantile, or manufacturing—mean trade, and trade means risk. If I buy shares in

Jones and Popkins' brewery, I become a brewer to the extent of my liabilities; and just as much a tradesman as though I invested my money in a grocer's shop, and carried on the business myself. I buy shares as I might buy the retail business: if either be well selected, and well carried on, the profits will be large; if otherwise, I shall in both cases lose my money. I am induced to do what I do by the hopes of having trade profits; but then I must at the same time undertake trade risks. It must also be borne in mind that when a private business is made into a company, there is always a presumption against it; for what man, realizing a large income, will hand over its sources voluntarily to a body of strangers? This objection does not apply to banks, finance, and discount companies, by reason of the enormous capital they require.

Having then, with sufficient care, selected my investment with a view to trade profits, and recognising the impossibility of avoiding trade risks, I do not go to sleep; I watch the proceedings of my directors; I attend the meetings of the company; I study its balance sheets; I vote at all elections; and I bear in mind that it is only by attending to business duties that business risks can be kept down. Lastly, I support the company with my credit and my confidence. I *will* not accept the 'operation' for the fall; and under such circumstances I may not only hope to make my investment a good one, but I shall rarely fail. This is an exemplification of the maxim—"Nothing venture, nothing have."

The Iron Duke's maxim applies to those who forget that trade profits imply trade risks. He would not have said to a young man about to establish himself in a retail business—" Put your two hundred pounds in Consols, and live on the interest, for high interest means bad security;" but he would have counselled rigid scrutiny, and then permitted legitimate adventure. Only, if a man chooses to become a tradesman, and then leaves the shop to take care of itself, the least he can expect is an unpleasant notice in the *Gazette*.

I will conclude this chapter by a return to its primary subject, and subjoin a most vivid and picturesque description of a scene during the panic of 1825. It is taken from the shorthand writer's notes of the evidence given by Mr. Richards, the Deputy-Governor of the Bank of England, before a Committee of the House of Commons; and it will in some respects remind those who were in the City during the panic of 1866 of what they saw at that time.

PANIC OF 1825. 167

"I think," says Mr. Richards, "it must have been in the autumn of 1825 that the Bank began very seriously to contemplate what would be the result of the speculations and of various circumstances that were going forward. That increased in October and November, when there continued to be a very great demand for gold, which I think began about April; and I believe it advanced down to the first Saturday in December. Not only the Bank, but, I believe, every man's mind connected with the City, was in an extreme state of excitement and alarm. I think I can recollect, on the first Saturday in December, having come home after a very weary and anxious day from the Bank, receiving a visit from two members of this committee and one of our bankers, at my own house, stating a difficulty in which a banking-house near to the Bank was placed. I will not assert it, but I believe they had gone so far as to take care of the clearing of that house that evening, so that it might fulfil its engagements. The object of that visit was to ascertain what would be my views upon the subject. I was called upon because the *Governor was particularly connected with the house of* Pole and Co., *by marriage and other circumstances of relationship.* After speaking upon the subject for some time, I was pretty sure that I

could answer for the firmness of the Bank; and I
ventured to encourage these gentlemen to hope
that, upon anything like a fair statement, the Bank
would not let this concern fall through. It was
agreed that upon the following morning (Sunday),
we should meet as many directors as I could get
together, with the three gentlemen who had called
upon me, at the house of one of them; and that in
the meantime some eminent merchants, friends of
the house, should also be called to the meeting to
assist with their opinion. We so met; and, after
hearing all the facts, which were collected in the
first instance by the bankers and merchants present, the directors authorized their chairman to say
that assistance should not be wanting. It was
agreed that £200,000 should be placed at the dis-
posal of Pole and Company the next morning, for
which the Bank was to receive, as securities, a
number of bills of exchange and notes of hand;
and over and above, a mortgage on Sir Peter Pole's
property, which was to ride over the whole. They
fought it through till Thursday or Friday pretty
manfully, and up to Saturday evening, when their
position was such, that without assistance of the
same eminent individuals who had taken part
before, the clearing would not have gone right.
Sunday passed: and on Monday morning the

storm began; and till Saturday night it raged with an intensity that it is impossible for me to describe. On Saturday night it had somewhat abated. The Bank had taken a firm and deliberate resolution to make common cause with the country as far as their humble efforts would go. In the following week things began to get a little more steady; and by the 24th, what with the one-pound notes which had gone out, and other things, people began to be satisfied; and then it was, for the first time in a fortnight, that those who had been busied in that terrible scene could recollect that they had any families who had some claim upon their attention. It happened to me not to see my children for that week."

CHAPTER XIII.

HOW THE NATIONAL DEBTS ARE TO BE PAID.

Necessity of the Payment—Taxation—How to be Arranged—Direct and Indirect—Argument in favour of each Income Tax—Excise and Customs—Balance in favour of Taxation, partly Direct and partly Indirect.

NATIONAL debts follow the same rule with regard to their payment as other obligations of the kind—they require to be defrayed out of national resources. Foreign debts are usually secured by hypothecating some sources of these revenues; but in our own country the whole burden falls on the general income, and is annually paid out of the amount collected by taxes. It is to be observed that no creditor of the Government can require the payment of his individual debt, he can only transfer it to another person, who will, in that case, become the creditor of the nation in his place, and receive his portion of the dividends. And here intervenes the connexion between the money market and the taxation of the country. If the debt be a national one, the payment of the interest becomes a national duty; and all who derive benefit from the results produced by the money lent to the nation are bound to take a part in that payment. Taxation, also, affects the money market directly and mechanically, as well as philosophically, for an unpopular or impolitic tax will cause a fall in the funds in direct proportion to its unpopularity or its impolicy.

Again, whatever is an evidence of the general welfare raises the price of the funds—and nothing can be a greater evidence of this than a surplus revenue—a deficit always lowers the current value, while a surplus income as invariably has the opposite effect. On this account the subject of taxation must not be omitted here, though it will require to be briefly treated.

We have arrived at the conclusion, that the purposes for which, among ourselves, taxation is imposed, are just and right. We come next to the questions, in what manner these public contributions should be levied? and who are the persons on whom the burden ought to fall?

Of these two questions, the latter must take precedence, because the manner of raising the public income is wholly determined by the consideration upon what classes it is intended to lay the burden.

If I wish to tax solely the rich, I must lay an

impost on all articles of luxury, and establish a property-tax of such a nature as to leave untouched small sums and small incomes. If I wish to tax chiefly the poor, I must tax the necessaries of life, and the wages of the workman. But it may be remarked, that no system of mere taxation can be devised by which the wealthy can be altogether exempted, and the poor alone burdened.

All that can be done towards this iniquitous and impolitic end is to make the poor man pay as much as the rich; and this would be effectually accomplished by taxing simply the *necessaries* of life; for as the rich man cannot consume more than the poor, so he would not be called upon to pay more.

I think it will hardly be denied that, as Government exists for the welfare of all, it has a claim upon all for support; and this will be the more evident in proportion as the right is recognised of universal *representation* (universal *suffrage* is another thing). No man is exempt from this claim simply because he is poor, for he, in return, makes his claim upon Government for protection in life and limb, in the exercise of his civil rights, and his religious duties. He requires to be sure of his wages, to be defended against invasions from abroad, and riots at home; and for these advantages he looks to the rulers of the country.

Universal taxation, therefore, *must* follow universal representation; and if the principles of pure justice were applied to the question, none would be more easily solved, for each would then be called upon to contribute in proportion to his ability. Not simply because he who has ten thousand pounds receives ten times as much protection as he who has but one thousand, nor solely on account of any arithmetical proportion whatever, but also because all men are stewards of that wealth which God has given, and which is *His;* they are bound as such, therefore, to distribute it. The duty of supporting Government is of divine authority, and men are under obligation to fulfil it according to what they have, and not according to what they have not.

The object of taxation, then, is to raise by the contributions of every member of the community a sum requisite for, and adequate to, the public service, and to arrange these contributions so that no one shall pay more or less than his share.

This is attempted to be done by two modes of taxation, direct and indirect.

Taxation is *direct* when a specific sum of money is demanded of the citizen for the use of the

Government. An income-tax, a property-tax, a land-tax, a poll- or capitation-tax, assessed taxes, legacy-duties, poor-rates, and rates of all kinds, are instances of direct taxation.

Corn-laws, excise, customs, and stamp-duties, are instances of indirect taxation.

It has been contended by some, that all taxation ought to be *direct*; by others, that it ought to be wholly indirect.

The advocates of direct taxation say that as property and persons alone require Government protection, so an income-tax which repays the one, and a capitation tax which defrays the expenses of the other, would be at once the fairest, the easiest to collect, and the least expensive in the collection of all imposts; and that therefore into these, all taxes should be commuted.

They further observe that direct taxation is by no means so unpopular as it is sometimes supposed; that men are willing to pay their contributions, when they are satisfied of the necessity, which all are now, and when they see the fairness of the assessment, which all then could understand.

They also contend that the negative benefits of direct taxation are yet greater than the positive, for in all indirect taxation the expense of collection is doubled: the interests of particular classes or trades are consulted, to the disadvantage of the rest, a new crime is created, that of smuggling, the moral evil of which it is very difficult to exhibit to the uneducated classes in its true light, and that the public revenues are diminished, without any corresponding benefit in return. Besides all these objections, indirect taxation interferes with the freedom of trade, and by its restrictions, limits and sometimes neutralizes the advantages which the industry of a country may obtain for its inhabitants.

The advocates for indirect taxation rest their defence on these points, they contend that—

1.—It reaches most easily all incomes, securing the contributions of all to the public need. It may be very difficult to obtain the payment of a few shillings by way of direct taxation from the labouring man; but it is very easy to lay a tax upon his bread, his beer, and his tea, which tax he cannot avoid paying, and does indeed pay unconsciously, and without a murmur.

2.—That it avoids the unpopular and apparently oppressive measure of demanding so much money as a direct payment for Government protection, and at the same time is free from the objection of encouraging falsehood and concealment, which an income-tax is sure more or less to occasion.

3.—That it involves the principle of protection, without which, as they allege, the agriculturist and manufacturer of our own country have no chance of success in contending with the more lightly-taxed foreigner.

Now, as all these arguments have their weight, and require to be taken into account (save the last, which is to be decided on other grounds, and has been considered in a separate chapter), we have to strike a balance of benefits and evils, and decide accordingly.

The theory which would commute all taxes into an income-tax and a capitation-tax would be a perfectly true one, were it possible for an income-tax to be levied on perfectly fair principles, and to reach accurately the incomes it professes to assess; but the first of these desiderata has not yet been so much as attempted, and all experience shows us that the latter is not to be expected.

Let it be supposed, however, that a fairly graduated income-tax were established, reaching *all* incomes, and enabling employers to pay for their workmen, while it did not press too heavily upon the larger incomes, it would still be necessary to create supplementary taxes to supply the deficiency—a growing deficiency, too—occasioned by the evasions of the tax.

Should this deficiency be made good by direct or by indirect taxation? Partly, without doubt, by the former; a few direct taxes on articles of luxury or ostentation—such as carriages, horses, dogs, armorial bearings, servants not employed in business—would be expedient, both as supplying the required sum and equalizing the irregularities of the greater and more universal tax.

A house-tax, if equitably levied, is perhaps as fair as any of these supplementary imposts, for few more accurate means exist of ascertaining the amount of any man's income than the manner in which he chooses to be lodged. Few taxes are, on the other hand, more noxious than a window-tax, its results being equally injurious to health, to taste, to art, to trade, and to comfort.

If, after all, any mode of indirect taxation should be considered needful in aid of the more direct mode, it should be levied on such subjects as are of sufficiently general use to produce a sum large enough for the purpose required, and which are yet not the absolute necessaries of life.

The argument against the *principle* of direct taxation, on the ground of its unpopularity, may be speedily disposed of. Men for the most part regard the matter in a purely utilitarian point of view, and are keen enough to perceive which system is really the most oppressive. If a Government which obliges me to pay seven pounds per annum in direct taxes does at the same time enable me to save ten pounds every year in the necessaries of life, I shall hardly be so foolish as to clamour against direct taxation, nor is it likely that the real state of the case can be hidden from the great mass of the nation. On the whole, the balance of argument is really in favour of the more direct method, while at the same time direct taxation could not be imposed to the extent which our necessities require; and there are also limits within which indirect taxation may at all times be permitted without disadvantage.

The last question is, Whether there be any probability of liquidating this debt? That it is desirable, no one can doubt; although, as its desirability consists in the decrease of taxation, every tax, either direct or indirect, which is remitted, has precisely the same effect on the amount demanded from the public, as though a portion of the debt, with its consequent burdens, were removed. There is, moreover, this advantage attending the removal of taxes, instead of liquidating portions of the debt, that those imposts which are most objectionable may be taken off in succession; and when no obnoxious taxes remain, then the surplus may be applied to the liquidation of the debt.

CHAPTER XIV.

GREAT FINANCIAL FAMILIES.

Great Financial Families—The Houses of Coutts—Payne and Smith—Jones Loyd—Lord Overstone—The Barings—Lord Ashburton—The Rothschilds—Original name Amschel—Origin of the name Rothschild—Nathan Rothschild.

A FEW anecdotes of distinguished financiers may tend to enliven the drier topics of monetary science :—

> "There is a tide in the affairs of men (says Shakspeare),
> Which taken at the flow, leads on to fortune."

The above oft-repeated truism has been signally exemplified in the history of the great banking-houses. We begin with the origin of COUTTS AND Co. The founder was William Coutts, a careful but enterprising merchant of Edinburgh, whose two youngest sons, James and Thomas, were brought up in business under the paternal eye, working daily at their respective desks. The former came to London at the age of twenty-five, and soon after undertook the business of a banker in the Strand, in the same house in which the business of the firm is at present carried on. His brother Thomas joined him in the enterprise; and after the death of James, which soon occurred, Thomas became the sole proprietor of the bank.

An instance of his inherent shrewdness has been recorded by Mr. Lawson, the historian of banking. In order to secure the co-operation of the heads of the leading banking-houses, it was his habit frequently to invite them to dinner. On one of these occasions, a guest remarked that a certain nobleman that day applied for a loan of £30,000, and had been refused. Mr. Coutts heard this, said nothing, but that same night he waited upon the nobleman in question, and requested a call from him at the banking-house the next morning. The invitation was accepted. Mr. Coutts received his visitor with much politeness, and offered for his acceptance the sum which he had asked for from the other house. Agreeably surprised, he exclaimed, "But what security shall I give you?" "I shall be satisfied with your lordship's I.O.U." was the reply. £10,000 was received, and £20,000 returned to open an account with the bank in his lordship's name. The £10,000 was soon repaid, and £20,000 more deposited in the care of the bank. High patronage began to flow into the firm, and among the new customers was, for a time, King George the Third.

The origin of the firm of Jones, Loyd & Co. was curious and romantic. The father of the present Lord Overstone, the Rev. Mr. Loyd, began his career as a Dissenting Minister in a small chapel at Manchester. One member of his congregation was a Mr. Jones, half banker and half manufacturer, whose daughter attended the ministry of the Rev. Mr. Loyd. Between the minister and the banker's daughter an attachment sprang up, and, despairing of obtaining the consent of Mr. Jones, they contracted a secret marriage. Mr. Jones, like a wise man, made the best of the case, and was reconciled to his reverend son-in-law; but, as he did not consider preaching to be a lucrative business, he proposed that Mr. Loyd should doff the gown and become a banker in partnership with himself. He yielded to this suggestion, and became one of the firm of Jones, Loyd & Co.

Mr. Loyd, as a banker, appears to have been the right man in the right place; his head was clear, his eye single, and his industry, combined with great talent for business, proved successful for many years, and he was succeeded by his son, Samuel

Jones Loyd, who was created a peer under the title of Lord Overstone.

The origin of the bank of Messrs. Barclay & Co., whose founders were linendrapers in Cheapside, is rife with interest. Mr. Lawson relates that on Lord Mayor's Day, 1760, George III. made a State visit to the City. There was, from political causes, some irritation among the people, and much tumult in the great thoroughfare between St. Paul's and the Bank, so that one of the horses in the royal carriage became restive, and the king and queen were in apparent danger. In this emergency David Barclay (a Quaker) rushed to the rescue, and, addressing the king, said—" Wilt thee alight, George, and thy wife Charlotte, and come into my house and see the Lord Mayor's show." The king with many of his family, like Nicholas the late Emperor of all the Russias, had a profound respect for the Society of Friends, he accepted the invitation of the draper, and went up to the first floor. The cavalcade having passed, the Quaker went through the ceremony of introduction, which, although opposed to formalities in general, David Barclay on this occasion minutely performed. " King George of England—Priscilla Barclay, my wife;" "Priscilla, my wife — George, King of England," &c. &c. On taking his leave the king most courteously invited the Quaker to visit him at the Palace of St. James's.

At the next levee David Barclay went to court with his son John. When the king saw them he threw aside the restraint of *etiquette*, and gave David a hearty shake of the hand. One of the king's inquiries to David was—" What do you intend to do with your son John? Let him come here, and I will find him good and profitable employment"—an offer civilly, and perhaps wisely, declined. It is necessary to state that the truth of this story has been disputed.

Soon after this interview he established his two sons, James and John, as bankers, in Lombard Street. The descendants of David Barclay subsequently became great brewers as well as bankers, and founded the world-renowned firm of Barclay and Perkins. The two great banking and brewing firms are, at the present time, composed almost entirely of the descendants of the linendraper of Cheapside who entertained George III.

Another private banking firm whose story is replete with interest, is that of Smith, Payne, and

Co., Lombard Street. This rich and important firm sprang into existence at Nottingham, at the beginning of the eighteenth century, Smith, the first—the *taproot* of all the other Smiths—like David Barclay, was a draper, and, being an obliging man, was well patronized, especially on market days, by the wives of the farmers from the country round about. When they had disposed of their chickens, eggs, and butter, they resorted to Smith's the draper to buy their linsey-wolsey gown-pieces, their tapes, neckerchiefs, and thread. Their husbands, after selling their corn and pigs, were wont to smoke their pipes in the draper's cozy back-parlour while their wives were making their purchases in the shop. There they would be joined by Mr. Smith, who could entertain them with the news of the day. One theme of conversation was often uppermost—how they should get safe home with their money; the outskirts of Nottingham being proverbially infested by footpads. Here had been the home of Robin Hood and Little John, and the frequent resort of Dick Turpin himself, so that there was old prescription for the then existing state of things.

The calculating head and the honest heart of Mr. Smith hit upon a plan to give security to the farmers, while it would bring credit and profit to himself. "I will keep your money," said he, "and what is more, I will keep an account of your market transactions; and then you can draw your cash or get goods from me, as it may best suit your interest and convenience." The plan was feasible, and it was acted upon at once. Mr. Smith was soon in possession of large sums of money, with which he could and did accommodate merchants and tradesmen in Nottingham. The interest for this money became a fruitful source of income, the profits being entirely his own. In time Mr. Smith became a regular banker. After his death his son extended his operations to Lincoln and to Hull. His grandson sought for and found a correspondent in London, who, like himself, was active and shrewd in all his dealings. This was Mr. Payne, with whom he entered into partnership, and hence arose the firm of Smith, Payne, and Co., near the Mansion-house, which still keeps its footing notwithstanding the all-absorbing influences of the Joint-stock Banks.

A still more important firm was that of
The Barings.
Their immediate ancestor was a Lutheran pastor

settled in England. His son, John Baring, established himself as a cloth manufacturer in Devonshire. He acquired a fortune, and left behind him four enterprising sons, of whom Francis, the second, devoted himself to banking. He speculated largely in Government loans, and subsequently became the friend and monetary adviser to Lord Shelbourn, the predecessor of Mr. Pitt. To secure the goodwill of this great banker, Mr. Pitt created him a baronet. He died in September, 1810, leaving a fortune of more than £2,000,000.

In the next generation we find Alexander Baring, the son of the late Sir Francis, placed at the head of the firm, and undertaking the greatest monetary operations ever effected by a single banker. Upon one occasion he lent to France the sum of £1,000,000, at five per cent., which freed France from the burden of 150,000 foreign troops which were occupying that country. Alexander Baring died at Longleat in Wilts, in 1848, after being elevated to the peerage as Lord Ashburton. The present head of the house is Thomas Baring, M.P. for Huntingdon since 1844. Parliament in the session of 1864 could count six Barings—one among the Lords, and five in the House of Commons. In the course of a century the descendants of the German pastor have risen to the highest political influences and become princes in the commercial world.

Thomas Guy, the founder of the hospital which bears his name, though not, strictly speaking, a banker, yet as a clever speculator and an extensive dealer in scrip, must have a passing notice on account of the incalculable benefits he has conferred upon the afflicted by the erection and endowment of that princely building, Guy's Hospital.

He was the son of a lighterman and coal-dealer in Horselydown, and was apprenticed to a bookseller in 1660. He opened a small shop at the corner of Lombard Street, where he made money by selling Bibles. Cool, calculating, and extremely parsimonious, his active mind was ever on the alert; and during the time of the South Sea Bubble, which engulphed thousands of families in ruin, though foreseeing the tremendous catastrophe which hung over the land, he purchased the scrip to the utmost of his means. When the price had risen to 1000 per cent. he sold out, and realized a profit to the extent of a million sterling. Towards the close of his life he grew more and more rapacious; but he, nevertheless, determined to risk the expenses of matrimony, and to take his maidservant to be his wife. The nuptials were arranged, when he ordered some slight repairs to be made on the pavement in the front of his shop; the intended wife, elated with her prospects, ordered the repairs in question to extend a few inches further than her master had directed. This so displeased the millionaire that he broke off the match and gave the whole of his property, by his will, for the foundation of an hospital upon the largest scale ever known. He likewise built a number of almshouses at Tamworth. He died December, 1724, in the eighty-second year of his age, having dedicated more money to charitable purposes than any other man upon record. Thus, out of the most swindling transaction of the age, rose up the most magnificent hospital that ever adorned the world.

We conclude this chapter with a brief account of THE ROTHSCHILDS.

In the centre of the city of Frankfort-on-the-Maine there is a dirty, narrow, unsightly, and most miserable street, called Juden Gasse (in English, Jew Lane); here, in fact, the whole race were imprisoned; they were not permitted to reside in any other part of the city, nor to move out of their dismal dwelling-place on Sundays or holidays, nor before a certain hour in the morning, nor after a certain hour at night. It was in this lane Meyer Amschel, the founder of the house of Rothschild, was born. He lost his parents at the tender age of eleven, after he had been at school but a few years, and he then marched off with his stick and a bundle over his shoulders to seek his fortune at Hanover, where he was employed as a clerk by a money-changer. He saved a trifle of money, married, and set up a shop as a dealer and collector of old coins; his sign was "THE RED SHIELD," from which circumstance he was called *Rothschild*. The one only object of his life was to get money, and this art he completely understood. The calamities of war made ready money scarce; nobles deposited their jewels, and freeholders mortgaged their estates—which they could never redeem—into the hands of Rothschild, often for small sums of money; suffice it to say that, in six years, he had amassed an enormous fortune. He died worth one million sterling, leaving a family of ten children, five sons and five daughters. The five sons surrounded the death-bed of their father, and each of them swore to act upon his will; this was, that they should enter into a co-partnership, and carry on the business of banking. Anselm, the eldest, was the nominal head, but Nathan, who inherited his father's talents, was the real chief of the firm. Eager to make money, and seeing the rising importance of the English money-market, Nathan left his home, and came to Manchester with eighty-four pounds in his pocket. He began business by lending small sums of money at extortionate interest; and at the end of five years (1803) he came to London with a sum of £200,000, and became a member of the Stock Exchange. He speculated in the public funds, where his eagle-eyed shrewdness and intuitive knowledge enabled him to realize immense profits.

At times, during the Peninsular War (1810), the Government was pressed for money to supply the heavy demands from the great Duke, and the exchequer was nearly empty; Nathan Rothschild having faith in the ultimate success of the British arms, often supplied the money. He purchased bills at a large discount, and made them over to the Government at par, and then furnished the money for redeeming them. This proved a splendid speculation. By employing a staff of agents abroad to collect all intelligence of a warlike nature, which was conveyed to him by carrier-pigeons, he was supplied with the news of victories and defeats long before they were known in Downing Street; and was thus prepared to make his bargains on "change." By means like these the wealthy Hebrew brought almost daily large sums into his coffers.

When Napoleon returned from Elba, 1815, Rothschild's anxiety knew no bounds. During those memorable one hundred days prior to the decisive Battle of Waterloo, he was in a fever of excitement. He went himself to the battle-field, and placed himself on the hill of Hougoumont, to watch the progress of the engagement, and there he remained until near sunset, on June 18th. When he beheld the French in full retreat, he saw that Waterloo was won for England, and wealth almost immeasurable for himself. He galloped off to Brussels, and from thence to Ostend. Next morning, by sunrise, he was opposite the coast of England; the waves were high, and the troubled sea moaning as though it were sounding a requiem for the thousands of the dead who had been sacrificed to quell the ambition of Napoleon, and to replace a Bourbon on the throne of France.

The great financier tempted a poor fisherman by an offer of £80 to carry him across from Ostend to Deal or to Dover, where he landed in safety, and having procured the swiftest horses to convey him on his journey to London, he artfully but most heartlessly contributed by his hypocritical forebodings to increase the gloom that hung over Threadneedle Street. "Blucher," he whispered, to a few of his friends, "has been routed at Ligny, and Heaven only knows what has become of Wellington!" The fall in the funds was tremendous.

Rothschild's known agents were all eager to sell, while his secret agents bought while there was a bit of scrip in the market. This panic continued until the truth came out, and then the funds rose faster than they had previously gone down. This strategic but most unjustifiable speculation enriched the house of Rothschild by a million sterling.

Having gained his first two million pounds, honours rained upon himself and the house he represented. Nothing was too large for his grasp, and nothing too small for his notice; while as to his compeers he could ride roughshod over them.

While investing the profits of ten millions and buying an estate for £115,000 with the premium of a single loan, he could calculate to a penny as to how much it would take to keep alive the clerks and their families in his employ. A rough, homely poet says—

> "The man may *last*, but never *lives*,
> Who much receives, and nothing gives;
> Whom none can love, whom none can thank—
> Creation's blot, Creation's blank."

THE END.

www.ingramcontent.com/pod-product-compliance
Lightning Source LLC
Chambersburg PA
CBHW020921230426
43666CB00008B/1524